WORSHIP for VITAL Congregations

Talitha Arnold

Anthony B. Robinson, Series Ed.

THE
PILGRIM
PRESS
Cleveland

The Pilgrim Press, 700 Prospect Avenue East,
Cleveland, Ohio 44115-1100
thepilgrimpress.com
©2007 Talitha Arnold

Biblical quotations are from the *New Revised Standard Version of the Bible*, ©1989 by the Division of Christian Education of the National Council of Churches of Christ in the U.S.A., and are used by permission.

 Printed in the United States of America on acid-free paper that contains post-consumer fiber.

Library of Congress Cataloging-in-Publication Data

Arnold, Talitha, 1953–
  Worship for vital congregations / Talitha Arnold.
      p. cm. -- (Congregational vitality series)
  Includes bibliographical references.
  ISBN 978-0-8298-1729-4 (alk. paper)
  1. Public worship. I. Title.
  BV15.A765 2007
  264--dc22
                                        2007043881

Contents

119798

Editor's Foreword

A guiding principle for this series of books, which are a part of the Congregational Vitality Initiative of the United Church of Christ, is that they are written by practitioners, people who actually do this work and do it with distinction. Talitha Arnold, pastor of the United Church of Santa Fe, New Mexico, fits the bill! Talitha is immersed in the life of a growing congregation, one that was a new church start twenty-five years ago. Under Talitha's leadership the congregation in Santa Fe has grown in every way: faith and focus, attendance and membership, giving and service, building and public witness. At the heart of it all is a worship life that is vibrant, authentic, biblical, spiritual, and creative. You will learn from Talitha as she has learned in her ministry and among God's people.

Talitha understands that worship is where congregational vitality begins. Worship is the beating heart of a vital congregation's life. In worship we dare to come into the presence of a powerful, redeeming, relentless, gracious, and liberating God. Here in worship we come into one another's presence. Here in worship we remember, week by week, who we are and whose we are.

But this pastor also understands that if the life of a vital congregation begins in worship, it does not end there. From worship, believers are sent forth into the world to be instruments of God's grace and presence in a broken and bruised world. Worship is not quiet time apart from the world. It is time apart with God, God's people, and God's story, so that we might engage the world God has created, which God loves, and which God is determined to redeem.

As you dive into these pages, you will also discover that this is a book that is deeply rooted in a two-fold context. For though worship touches the eternal, it is set in a particular time and a particular place. Throughout Talitha's book, the feel and features of the Southwest are evident, even palpable. Rivers, desert, Native American stories, Hispanic shrines, sagebrush, and wind are all here to feel, to smell, to hear. The lesson is clear: learn from the place where God has put you! Look and listen for God in your particular setting.

The second aspect of Talitha's two-fold contextual approach to worship is that this book does grow out of the life of a particular congregation, the United Church of Santa Fe in New Mexico. It reflects the hopes and trials, the struggles and triumphs of that congregation which has bloomed in the desert. Does this particularity limit the usefulness of this book for you in another setting? I am sure it does not. We get to the universal and to broader application by way of the specific and the particular.

So enjoy the vivid congregational and Southwest context of this rich text. May it stir into flame the embers of vitality that are there in the life of your congregation! Use it with your Worship Team, Worship Board, Church Council, or staff. Read it with other clergy or lay leaders and watch for the sparks from the burning fire of vital worship!

Anthony B. Robinson, Series Editor

Acknowledgments

From start to finish, worship is a communal endeavor, and I have been blessed throughout my life to have been a part of vital worshipping communities, including the ones that nurtured and challenged me as a young person (Neighborhood Congregational Church in South Phoenix and First Congregational Church in Tempe, Arizona) and those I've had the privilege to serve (Tempe First Congregational; Yale University's Battell Chapel and The Church of Christ at Yale; First Church of Christ in Middletown, Connecticut; and the United Church of Santa Fe). In all those settings, I have been fortunate to have colleagues who, along with wonderful lay leaders, shared the delight in what's possible when people come together in worship to offer their very best to God and their brothers and sisters. In particular, it's been a blessing to work through the years with gifted and committed clergy, including Gary Reyes, Bill Bliss, Paul Gaston, Mary Greene, Russ Mueller, Bill Roberts, John Vannorsdall, and music staff, including Jacquelyn Helin, Catherine Robinson, Donna Clark, Heidi Hermansen, Evelyn Hickox, Ken Knight, Lin Raymond, Krista River, Solveig Solem, Sally Strong, karen Watson, Kent Wilson, and Angie Witter, and program and support staff, including Janice Ballard, Gerry Bushrow, Linda Drapela, Sandra Hareld, Drew Martin, Ella Natonabah Jones, and Carol Van Deusen. I am also indebted to clergy and lay leaders in the wider United Church of Christ and other faith traditions whose perspectives and encouragement have enriched my ministry, particularly my understandings of worship.

The chapters that follow were read in a variety of incarnations by several people who not only offered good advice, but invaluable encouragement: Joan Forsberg, Jacquelyn Helin, Rhea Higgins, Craig Hoopes, Doug Loving, Kirste Mulholland, Tony Robinson, Cherry Rohe, Gary and Karen Salman, Vickie Sewing, and LeAnne Summers. I also offer special thanks to Drew Martin, without whose editorial assistance this book would never have made it to press. In addition, conversations with our Worship Teams and other choirs and other musical groups, Church Councils, Liturgical Arts Teams, especially Darlene Garton, Dorothy Mendelson, Gene Law, and Larry Hays, and other lay leaders provided ongoing insights through the years, as did conversations with Trudy Weaver Miller and other staff of the Berkshire Choral Festival.

I am also grateful to Kim Sadler of The Pilgrim Press, series editor Anthony Robinson, and copyeditor Amy Wagner, for their guidance and patience when the pastoral needs of the church took precedent over writing.

I could not write a book on worship without acknowledging the debt I owe to Yale Divinity School. When I started YDS in 1976, I never intended to go into parish ministry nor lead worship on a regular basis. But the depth and diversity of the community's worship life persuaded me to say yes to the call. Thanks both to classmates and faculty such as Margaret Farley, Joan Forsberg, Peter Hawkins, Carl Holladay, Luke Timothy Johnson, Leander Keck, Henri Nouwen, Jeffery Rowthorn, and Letty Russell. It was the best training I could have had for being a leader of worship in the last part of the twentieth century and these opening years of the twenty-first.

A similar debt is owed to the people of the United Church of Santa Fe. Their commitment to engaging the lively Word of God shaped the vital worship upon which much of this book is based, and I am deeply grateful. It is to the members, friends, and staff of United, present and past, that this book is dedicated.

Finally, a great thanks to Chris Wismer and Scott Swearingen, river runners par excellent, and the other traveling companions of the journey who made this book possible.

▼

Introduction

When Does Worship Begin?

When does worship begin for you?"
The person asking the question was an architect named Craig Hoopes. The people he was addressing were the Building Committee for the United Church of Santa Fe, in our first meeting to develop a master building plan for our congregation.

The journey to that meeting had been a long one. United was seventeen years old, and I had been the minister for ten of those years. The congregation had started in the late 1970s as part of the United Church of Christ's "New Initiatives in Church Development" whose goal was to plant new churches in fast-growing areas, like the Southwest.

By the mid-1980s, United, like many new church starts, had hit rocky ground, particularly in terms of finances (the ninety-member congregation had a half-million dollar debt and a $60,000 yearly mortgage payment); staff (there was none); and building (a leaky roof, no room for children, and other construction problems).

Like many UCC congregations, there was ongoing concern for balancing our outreach ministries and financial support for the wider community with "taking care of ourselves," meaning fixing the roof, paying off the debt, developing staff, and building adequate space.

By 1997, we had done much of that, along with increasing outreach giving threefold. The congregation had grown to two hundred people. Now we were bursting at the seams with a sanctuary that seated less than a hundred, two bathrooms, and a single education room for toddlers to teens.

After two years of feasibility studies and facilities-use surveys, we moved a "temporary modular unit" (a.k.a., trailer) onto our 3½ acres for nursery space. The neighbors wouldn't tolerate our temporary solution for long, so if we were to become a viable congregation, we needed to develop a master plan for building.

After interviewing three architects, we chose Craig largely because he had renovated a chapel for an order of Carmelite nuns and done theater design. But at that first meeting, my mind wasn't on sacred space. Instead it was filled with more immediate questions. Where were we going to put the babies and the bathrooms? How were we going to pay for it all?

We introduced ourselves. Then Craig asked his first question: "When does worship begin for you?" It caught me off guard. Why was he asking about worship when we had more urgent things to worry about? By the grace of God, I didn't voice my surprise or irritation. Instead I sat back and listened to what the Building Committee had to say. It took them a few minutes to readjust their thinking from the practical and pressing. When *does* worship begin? For some it was when they entered the sanctuary and heard the prelude. For others, it was after the announcements, when we took time to breathe God's Spirit. A truthful young mother said worship began when her children left for Children's Ministry. For still others, worship began when they turned off the main street to the one that led to the church.

Then the conversation really took off. Over the next hour, we didn't talk nuts and bolts. Instead the committee talked about worship—when it begins, what it involves, why we do it, where we hope it leads us.

We shared what was important to each of us in worship, whether at United or elsewhere. We discussed how our worship life had changed, even over our short history, from gathering on Sunday mornings in a local restaurant to worshipping in our own sanctuary with its adobe wall and turquoised-tiled acequia. We explored the essentials of worship that continued through those changes—the feel of community, the commitment to a lively exploration of God's Word, the spirited singing even when we didn't have a pianist.

By the meeting's end, we still hadn't determined where babies would go nor discussed the budget. But thanks to Craig's question, we had talked about the most important part of our life and ministry: worship. In the words of a Jeffery Rowthorn hymn, we had, "amid the cares that claimed us, held in mind eternity."[1]

Craig's question reminded me of the advice Reuben Sheares gave me ten years before when I said yes to becoming United's Pastor. I had served on the Office for Church Life and Leadership Directorate when Reuben was the executive director and I was a young associate minister for a church in Connecticut. I couldn't have asked for a better mentor in ministry.

When I moved from First Church, Middletown, Connecticut, to the United Church of Santa Fe, New Mexico, I went from a three hundred-fifty-year-old, seven-hundred-member congregation with a half-million dollar endowment to one that was seven years old, had ninety members, and had that pesky half-million dollar debt. The Connecticut church had four choirs, a beautiful organ, two pianos, and a sanctuary filled with color and light. United of Santa Fe had no regular choir, couldn't afford a Sunday accompanist, and gathered in a sanctuary that seated less than one hundred. The whole church was smaller than some members' houses.

Thanks to the leadership of a strong founding minister, Marty Baumer, United got off to a good start, but after she left, the congregation went through two years of difficult transition and came close to splitting. By the time I came, they were dealing with all the aforementioned issues, along with trying to make the transition from being a "house" or "family" church to a larger size and stage of life.

United's administrative, financial, and leadership challenges were matched by its spiritual ones. When I left New England for New Mexico, I went from where the Congregational branch of the UCC was born to one where the closest UCC congregation was fifty miles away and the dominant religious cultures were a mix of Hispanic Catholic, Native American, and Anglo New Age. In addition, say "United Church of Christ" in the Southwest, and people confuse you with Church of Christ, Unitarian, or Unity.

United's worship life had been rooted in UCC and Reformed Protestant traditions, but in the two years after the founding minister left, worship was led by a number of different people with a variety of styles, experiences, and theology. That mix was complicated by the fact that while many people came to Santa Fe (and still do) to seek spiritual enlightenment, they are often suspicious of and even hostile to anything resembling organized religion, especially Christianity. At times, United's worship life reflected that suspicion. The first time we welcomed new members, another ordained minister in the congregation told me I should rethink using the "Re-affirmation of Baptismal Vows" from the United Church of Christ's *Book of Worship* because it felt, in his words, "too Christian for this congregation."

Lack of space, building problems, disagreements over outreach giving vs. paying the mortgage, wanting to grow but fearing change, developing leadership after two years of transition. It felt overwhelming. I didn't have a clue as to where or how to address all those concerns.

So I called Reuben. He listened patiently to my fears. Then he said, "Remember, Talitha, worship is the key. Your preaching is the key. You get one shot at them once a week. That one hour of worship will shape their lives, their faith, and their life together more than anything else you do. Keep it central. Don't take it for granted. Give it your absolute best."

That's what I and this church community have tried to do ever since. Over the last twenty years, in the midst of raising money and developing Children's Ministries, building staff and building Habitat Houses, fixing roofs and fixing meals for the homeless shelter, Reuben's words about worship have been the plumb line for our ministry here at United. We try to keep it central, and we try to give it our absolute best.

Some of the focus on worship has been born of necessity. We've had to make countless decisions about our worship life, from determining our primary instrument (piano or organ) to the type of seating in an expanded sanctuary (pews or chairs). Whether it's through creating new banners, choosing a new hymnal, finding ways to include children in "Big Church," or hiring new music staff, we've talked time and again about what we do in worship, why we do it, how we do it, and what it means.

Over the years, we've also expanded our understanding of being a worshipping community. We've added a number of special services: Mardi Gras, a "Rite of Separation" for our confirmands and their parents, a sunrise service on Easter. Sometimes we developed new rituals in traditional services, like Ash Wednesday, to offer new meaning for persons who may have experienced such worship as punitive or condemning in other settings. Thanks to our children's and youth leaders, the younger members of the congregation gather for "Children's Church" during the school year and in the Creation Awareness Center during the summer. To meet a need for a more contemplative experience, we offer an early morning prayer service during Lent and a monthly midweek "Service of Silence and Song."

We've adapted worship for the context in which we live. Celebrating Thanksgiving in Santa Fe, where Native Americans have lived and prayed for a long time, is a different experience than in New England where churches are named "Pilgrim" and "Plymouth." For several years, we have joined with other faith traditions for services such as Las Posadas (the journey of Mary and Joseph to find shelter) or Earth Day celebrations.

We have also developed special services for special needs. Like churches, synagogues, and mosques around the world, we gathered for worship the night of September 11, 2001, and in the weeks that followed to hold our country and our world in prayer. Two summers ago, in the midst of a terrible drought, we hosted an interfaith prayer service, where people were invited to pray not only for rain, but also for the wisdom and compassion to use it carefully and justly.

On the eve of the 2004 presidential election, we held a service of "Prayers for Wisdom and Justice" that included readings from Caesar Chavez, Martin Luther King Jr., and Suffragette Carrie Chapman Cott, and concluded with "America the Beautiful." The Sunday service after Katrina hit, we sang Dixieland songs and blessed a moving van filled with supplies that our youth minister was driving to an evacuation center in Texas.

As you can tell, we've focused a lot on worship at United It brings the community together, expands our vision, and gives us what we need for the ministry God calls us to do.

Besides, it's fun. On the advice of a clergy colleague who told me early on to "dream big and celebrate often," we've developed some special ways of doing that: "A Roof Blessing" when it was finally repaired; "A laying on of hands" for the new piano that featured the church's pianists, from a six-year-old beginner to a Steinway artist. We've gathered for ground breakings for building projects, and when the permits didn't come through in time, turned them into ground blessings. When we got the trailer for temporary nursery care, we blessed the space, gave thanks to God, and prayed for the little ones who would be cared for there.

Keeping worship the center of our life at United means that joy and hope are usually found there, too, since they are a primary purpose of worship, perhaps the only true purpose. As Frederick Buechner writes, "A Quaker Meeting, a Pontifical High Mass, the Family Service at First Presbyterian, a Holy Roller Happening—unless there is an element of joy and foolishness in the proceedings, the time would be better spent doing something useful."[2]

The time we have taken to develop the worship life of the church has been time well spent. I believe it has transformed the life and ministry of the congregation and also individual lives. A young man from the congregation, currently in seminary, writes of his experience of worship, "Attending worship services at United gave me a view of church as both comforting and challenging. It helped me understand the role of religion as potentially positive and a way of bringing people together.

"It's always compelled me to be a better person," he continues, "and I'm thankful for it."[3]

Like the young man, there is not a day when I am not grateful to people like Reuben Sheares and his "plumb line" advice to a young minister years ago or Craig the architect who reminded me what's important. I am equally grateful to many others who have taught me and shown me what worship can do in the life of a community and in our lives as individuals.

Despite the challenges of deadlines and rewrites, I am also appreciative of Tony Robinson's invitation to do this book and for his vision in conceiving the Congregational Vitality series. Midway through my ministry, it made me stop and remember why I do what I do. It is therefore with deep gratitude that I offer what follows in these pages about vital worship.

I offer it also with more than a bit of fear and trembling. To write a book about worship in our time is to enter a minefield of argument. Contemporary vs. traditional. Praise music vs. hymns. Cross or no cross. Pews vs. theater seats. Printed bulletins or big screens. There's not an element of worship that isn't open to debate.

To write a book about worship for the United Church of Christ is even more daunting, given the diversity within our denomination and our allegiance to congregational autonomy. During my tenure as chair of the OCLL Directorate in the mid-1980s, the *Book of Worship* was published. I marveled at how the staff and committee honored our varied worship practices of the UCC, along with the two-thousand-year-old Christian history of worship, and blended them into a coherent understanding and resource for worship in the Reformed tradition.

I was also surprised by the resistance of many clergy to the *Book of Worship*. It wasn't a *Book of Common Prayer*, as in the Episcopal Church, that bound a church to one form of worship. The services were meant to be "adopted and adapted" by local congregations to meet their particular needs and styles. Yet the book was not always greeted with open arms—or minds.

In my youthful enthusiasm for OCLL's efforts, I asked the leader of a large UCC congregation what he thought of it. "Fine," he responded curtly, "if you want to be a Greek Orthodox. All those rites and rituals. That's not Congregational."

I can imagine there are those who will read this book and say it's not "UCC" enough or inclusive enough. It certainly won't be in-depth enough. From Moses to Paul, Augustine to Evelyn Underhill, people have been writing about worship for millennia. One is well-advised to enter that company with more than a few butterflies—and caveats to the reader.

I certainly know this book is not the last word on worship. I hope it is a helpful word for both clergy and lay leaders in congregations. I pray also that it is an honest and truthful word, one that is faithful to God and also to the tradition and faith understandings of the United Church of Christ and the wider Christian tradition.

Most of all, I hope that what follows will tell of the passion I have for worship. I can't think of a greater privilege than to help design experiences that lead people closer to the mystery we call God. The opportunity to think about, plan, collaborate on, create, and lead regular public worship makes all the other tasks—stewardship campaigns, strategic planning, building maintenance, committee meetings, and pastoral care—worth doing.

When worship works, whether it's a regular Sunday service or a special anniversary, offered in the light of Christmas Eve or the shadows of Maundy Thursday, there is no greater joy in the world.

When it doesn't work, doesn't connect, isn't infused with the Spirit, gets bogged down in details, or simply falls flat, there is no greater sadness.

Perhaps the ideas in this book can help "make it work."

One last word. I write what follows as pastor in the service of a local church. In that role, I know—as you who are reading it may also well know—how difficult it can be to find the time to think creatively about worship, much less re-envision or revitalize ongoing practices.

A friend and colleague watched me between services one Sunday, as I fielded the usual myriad of questions and concerns (where the toilet paper was for the women's room, hearing that someone's husband was in the hospital, learning the ushers had run out of bulletins). "Being a parish minister," she said, shaking her head, "is like being nibbled to death by ducks."

I don't want to add one more voracious duck to your already sizeable "to do" list (e.g., "visit the sick, stock the bathrooms, raise the budget, create vital worship"). Rather I hope this book will commend you in what you are already doing and help you remember why you believe worship is important. May it encourage you in your work as a worship leader and offer ways of going about that work that might deepen, broaden, and revitalize worship in your life and in the lives of the people you serve.

One

The River of Life

We can never sneer at the stars, mock the dawn or scoff at the totality of being. Sublime grandeur evokes unhesitating, unflinching awe. Away from the immense, cloistered in our own concepts, we may scorn and revile everything. But standing between earth and sky, we are silenced by the sight.

—Abraham Heschel[1]

Because this is a book about worship, one might assume its genesis was in a church, with rites and rituals, hymns and Scripture.

But that's not where this book began. You see, there's this river . . .

In the summer of 2006, I took an eighteen-day raft trip down the Colorado River through the Grand Canyon. We put our five rafts in at Lee's Ferry a few miles below Glen Canyon Dam, and took them out 225 miles later at Diamond Creek on the Walapai Indian Reservation. The trip was organized by a good friend who had run the Colorado four times. Our group included a dozen long-time friends who had rafted, hiked, and explored the West as young adults, and a couple others, like myself, who were new to the river.

As a native Arizonan, I had seen pictures of the Grand Canyon all my life. I've hiked it three times, once rim to rim, but had never run the river nor explored the side canyons. My delight at the chance to finally do a river trip was matched only by my anxiety as the least experienced in boats and rivers.

During those eighteen days, we rafted through rock that ranged from two million to almost two billion years old. We navigated the largest rapids in America and hiked to waterfalls and rock falls. We slept under night skies starting with the Milky Way, then the full moon, and back to the Milky Way by journey's end.

Along the way, the river veterans shared their stories of other trips and their knowledge of particular rapids and campsites. We talked about those who had gone before us. John Wesley Powell, the one-armed Civil War veteran and son of a Methodist minister, who led the first expedition of the entire canyon, with ten men in four wooden dories they rowed backward. Georgie Clarke, a former Hollywood actress, who lashed huge rafts together to take tourists on the ride of their lives. Two college boys from Southern California (where else?), who floated down the 225 miles in Mae West life jackets dragging cases of beer and beef jerky behind them.

Such stories made me grateful for our journey and especially our leader. They also reminded me of the courage, fear, and foolhardiness of those who had run the river before, which put my own fear, foolhardiness, and courage into perspective.

At times, the conversation ran deeper. One friend recalled his last time on the river when he hiked out at midpoint because his father was dying. On this trip, one person was marking the one-year anniversary of her divorce; another grieving the breakup of a longtime relationship.

We shared times for which we had no words, when we discovered places where the combination of rock, wind, and water had created canyons of unfathomable beauty. Times when the first light of dawn transformed a dark rock wall into layers of soft color or when a day's last light bathed the world in rose and gold.

Sometimes we glided through still water and deep silence, when speaking even a single word would have been a travesty. Other times creation spoke for us, like the afternoon a thunderstorm rumbled through the eon-old rock of the canyon. I didn't go on the river trip to write about worship. To be honest, I wanted to get away from everything related to work, including weekly worship—or at least the weekly worries about getting the bulletin done, having enough ushers, making sure childcare was covered.

But despite my intentions, the parallels between running the Colorado River through the Grand Canyon and developing the worship life of a congregation kept surfacing. From the sense of awe and mystery evoked by the

Canyon (just like good worship) to the perspective on time offered by ancient fossils and even older rock (like worship's perspective of eternity) to the stories we shared of river runners who had gone before (like the biblical characters) to the camaraderie of sharing life, thanks, and awe (like being a part of a worshipping community), the river trip offered lesson after lesson about worship.

That should not have been a surprise. From the four rivers of Eden to John's final vision of the River of Life in Revelation, rivers flow through our biblical faith. The biblical story takes place in a desert land, and rivers are sources of life—literally. They are also places of transformation, as Jacob discovered at the River Jabbok, and of blessing, as Jesus experienced at the Jordan.

The Colorado River in the Grand Canyon offered me such life, transformation, and blessing. The trip was a chance to get away from work, but paradoxically, it renewed my vision of the core of that work: *worship*. The time on the river helped me get beyond my everyday worries about worship and remember what is truly important in worship, namely, in Evelyn Underhill's classic definition, "the response of the creature to the Eternal."[2]

I also realized on the journey that rivers, especially desert rivers, are good metaphors for the importance of vital worship in our congregations. When a river flows free and full, it nurtures all kind of life along its banks—desert willows and grasses, birds that nest in the bushes and trees, collared lizards, big horn sheep, beaver, deer, and yes, rattlesnakes and a mountain lion or two.

Step a few yards away from a desert river, and that life can't survive in the hard rock and sand. In the same way, life dries up when as individuals or faith communities we get too far away from the source of life God offers us in worship.

In the chapters that follow, I use the river journey to talk about vital worship in the life of a congregation. I do so not because of my personal adventure, but because I hope the river metaphor can offer insights into some of the essentials of vital worship—e.g., understanding why we do it, paying attention to its structure and rhythm, finding ways to keep it vital.

The Grand Canyon trip also offered one more lesson that, I believe, is critical to any conversation about Christian worship these days.

What makes the Canyon grand is not just the mile-deep central chasm that cuts down eons of rock, but also the 250 miles of side canyons, each one carved by the same forces of time, wind, and water and each one unique.

There's Silver Spring, a narrow slot canyon of red granite where the roar of a waterfall drowns out any conversation. Further down is Blacktail, a dry gorge of multilayered sandstone, deepening shadows, and a silence as profound as any cloister. Elves Chasm, a moss-covered playground of waterfalls and swimming holes, where our laughter rang through the splashing waters. Every canyon with different colors, sounds, and even smells (the dry air of Blacktail, the moist cool feel of Elves Chasm).

Midway through the trip, I realized these side canyons, each with its own sense of mystery and beauty, offered a way to think about worship in our diverse tradition and time. Whether its sounds were joyous or hushed, its colors brilliant or subdued, each canyon had been shaped by the same forces of water and wind and each led to the Colorado River. Each let us, in Rabbi Heschel's words, stand between heaven and earth and "be silenced by the sight."[3] Yet each canyon was different from all the others.

Like those canyons, the diverse expressions of Christian worship are shaped by the same force of God's presence and God's story. They can lead us to the timeless Source we call God, while evoking their own particular sense of mystery, power, and beauty. And like the Grand Canyon itself, what makes Christian worship grand is that profound diversity.

Of course there's one important difference. To my knowledge, no canyon ever thought it was *the* best expression of God's mystery, power, and imagination. Nor has one canyon ever said to another: "You're not doing it right."

The same cannot be said about many conversations concerning Christian worship. The so-called "worship wars" seem to break out in all settings of the church, and across all denominational lines. The arguments often seem focused more on issues of style and taste in worship, especially music, than on the *essence* of worship. Debating such issues can drain our congregations of the energy and focus needed to develop truly vital worship. At the same time, not assessing or exploring worship results in worship that is either stagnant or shallow or both, not unlike a river that's been damned up.

So how to get beyond the "worship wars"? How also to keep from getting nibbled to death by the ducks of detail in worship planning? In a word, how to know what really matters in worship?

To start, let's take a look at "what" worship is.

Two

What Is Worship?

She called them "beauty attacks." One of the women on the river trip sometimes stopped in the middle of a hike through a canyon and would just stand, looking around her. Other times, she would lie down and look up, or sit for an hour in silence. Once when someone asked her if she was okay, why she wasn't hiking on, she simply responded, "I'm having a beauty attack."

It was a pretty secular group that got into those boats in early June. All of us had grown up in faith traditions—Jewish, Hispanic Presbyterian, Mormon, Hispanic Catholic, Irish Catholic, Seventh Day Adventist. The group included a daughter of a Lutheran minister, another of a Mennonite minister, and the son of a Presbyterian pastor. One woman, raised Italian Catholic, had worked in India and knew Hindu meditations. But now as adults only one person besides me was a part of any faith community.

Still they knew when to stand in awe of something and how to say thanks to the universe for such beauty. They also knew they weren't the center of that universe. For each of us, those days of being immersed in eternity, from the first light of every dawn through every night of stars and moon, was a pretty worshipful experience.

But it wasn't worship. Awe-inspiring, yes. An experience of the Eternal, definitely. Ritual and a sense of community, yes. In short, the journey was deeply worshipful—but it wasn't worship. Not even those times in the rapids when we frequently invoked the name of God or Jesus or both.

But if an experience that inspiring isn't worship, then what *is* it? Is worship only what happens in church? Does the use of only certain songs and settings constitute worship?

No. Worship is not defined by a particular style, liturgical practice, music, or architecture. All of those are means to an end—the experience of and response to the Eternal. They help us worship, for they are ways to express praise, connect to the Divine, be filled with the Spirit, and offer our lives back to God. But they are *practices* of worship, not the *essence* of worship, and certainly not the object of worship—though sometimes we make them so.

Then what is worship? Here's a possible definition I've developed:

> Worship is the conscious, communal, concrete, and covenantal act of connecting with the eternal mystery and power we call God. It is a human creation, rooted in human cultures. In Christian worship we experience God's mystery and power not only as the life-giving Creator, but also in the life-transforming Christ, and the life-empowering Holy Spirit.

Worship Is a Conscious Act

The American composer Randall Thompson's "Alleluia" is a favorite of many church choirs. Beginning softly in unison, the five-minute piece uses only one word throughout: "Alleluia." It divides into parts, weaving the "Alleluias" in and out, up and down the musical scale, builds to its climax, comes back down to one last hushed "Alleluia," and ends with a whispered "Amen."

A friend once told me about Thompson's inspiration for the work. According to her, the composer believed that the whole universe was *always* singing "alleluia." All we needed to do was find our voice and sing along.

Thompson the composer may have affirmed all creation is always singing "alleluia," but Thompson the choral conductor would have probably agreed that it takes a bit more than simply opening our mouths to sing his "Alleluia." We have to hear that "alleluia" in the midst of the world's noise. We must decide that singing is what we want to do with our mouths, instead of other things—like eating, speaking, yawning, or kissing. With all the other words we use everyday—"Dear Sir or Madam," "How much does it cost?" "Let me check my calendar"—we must decide if "alleluia" is worth our time to say or sing.

All creation may be singing "alleluia" all the time, just like God is present all the time, no less in our everyday lives than in a chorus of "alleluias" or a trip in the Grand Canyon. What's different, of course, is our consciousness of it. Worship is an intentional act designed to let God get our attention and to let ourselves respond.

Yes, there are certainly times when God still manages to break through to reveal a new truth or overcome us with the colors of a sunset or a child's smile. But worship acknowledges that the relationship between God and us, as with any relationship, is a two-way street. We have a responsibility to nurture and develop it. God keeps showing up in our lives, be it in the beauty of a starry night or the next breath we take. We're called to show up, too. Countering the distractions of our world, worship is the conscious setting aside of sacred space and sacred time to be in relationship with the sacred Source of life.

Worship Is a Concrete Act

If we want to sing "Alleluia," we have to practice it. We also have to practice the presence of God. Worship helps us do that. Through rituals and symbols, it provides a structure for the experience of the Eternal and also for our response. The rhythm of worship, its songs and silences, and its specific elements (e.g., call to worship, invocation) help us focus and prepare to experience God's presence. The Scripture reading and the preached Word provide an understanding of that presence. The prayers and offering that follow invite us to respond with our lives, praise and petitions, and resources.

Liturgy is literally the "work of the people," and worship requires our active participation. Even in those parts led by others (e.g., Scripture, sermon, anthem), we are not passive recipients but active listeners, invited to reflect on what we are hearing. In the times of silence when it seems like nothing is happening, we are invited to empty ourselves to receive God's Spirit, to "wait on the Lord to renew our strength."

Worship is never "religious entertainment" performed by the people up front for our inspiration, edification, or amusement. Instead worship always seeks to engage the whole congregation in the lively Word and power of God.

Worship Is a Communal Act

No one voice can capture the full harmony of the heavenly "Alleluia." We need the community to help carry the tune. As one parishioner said, "I can sing hymns by myself, but I usually need someone to help me remember the verses I forgot."

Worship is communal because we need the wisdom and insights of others. "The worshipper, however lonely in appearance," Evelyn Underhill writes, "comes before God as a member of a great family; part of the Communion of Saints, living and dead."[1]

Worship is also communal because no one individual can fully embody the Divine Image in which we are all created. "Sing of colors," proclaims the Mexican folk song "De Colores." "Sing of colors that shine from God's face, many colors that tell us God's love to recall."[2]

Biblical models for worship demonstrate that communal nature. Joshua summoned the tribes of Israel to worship at Shechem, and Jesus gathered his disciples in the Upper Room for a last Passover. In his Revelation of God's realm, John of Patmos first saw countless angels, then the elders, then a vast throng of all peoples, tribes, nations, and tongues, all singing and praising together. Even seemingly solitary Isaiah was part of a greater worshipping community composed of the six-winged seraphim flying around and singing, "Holy, Holy, Holy."

Worship Is a Covenantal Act

We see that most clearly in those times in worship that are focused on covenant-making—baptism, confirmation, receiving new members, installing the new church council. Parents, confirmands, or new officers stand before the congregation and say "yes" to questions about their faith and life as Christ's disciples.

But all worship reminds us of the covenant God has made with all creation. We sing of God's faithfulness and our "trust in the Lord." We share the tangible symbols of God's new covenant in the bread and the cup. Worship also gives us ways to keep our part of that covenant, by sharing our gifts in the time of offering or our prayers of commitment to be a "new people of love and justice."

Again, the biblical models of worship underscore its covenantal nature. At Shechem, Joshua reminded the gathered tribes how God brought them out of bondage, cared for them in the wilderness, gave them the law so they could live together, and led them into the promised land. Then Joshua told them, "Choose this day whom you will worship, whom you will serve" and he sets up a stone as visible sign of that covenant (Josh 24:15). For Isaiah in the Temple, the sight of the most Holy God showed him how far he and his people had strayed from their covenant. "Woe is me! I am lost and my people are lost," the young man cried (Isa 6:5). But even his uncleanliness didn't make God break the covenant. Instead God offered cleansing and commissioned Isaiah to call the people back into right relationship.

26

In his last Passover meal with his disciples, Jesus used ritual food—the lamb shank, haroseth, bitter herbs—to remind them what God had done for their ancestors in slavery. Then he used the bread and the cup to give them a new covenant to remember from that night forward. In our worship, we are invited to remember and share in that same covenant.

Worship Is a Cultural Act

Worship seeks to connect us to the eternal and transcendent God. It is also a human creation, developed and experienced by a particular group of people in a specific time and place. Worship takes place in the midst of human cultures, and thus expresses the limits and differences within the human community.

The varied songs, prayers, and rituals of biblical worship represent such differences, whether in the assembled tribes of Joshua's time of Exodus, the exiled nation of Israel in Isaiah's age, the Jewish community under Roman rule in Jesus' day, or the Greek and Roman world of John's Revelation.

The relationship of worship to culture is a complex one. The 1996 Nairobi Statement on Worship, coming out of the World Council of Churches' gathering, affirms four aspects of worship's embodiment in culture: transcultural, contextual, countercultural, and cross-cultural. [3]

As Jesus reminded the Samaritan woman, worship is *transcultural* because God as Creator, Christ, and Holy Spirit transcends all cultures and human disagreements about the where, when, and how of worship.

At the same time, a community's worship takes place in the *context of a particular culture*, be it first-century Samaria or the twenty-first-century U.S. Southwest, in an "Emerging Church" of twenty-somethings or an established congregation of Sun City retirees. Congregations and leaders must also decide about the relationship of their worship to the mix of cultures around them. Should Christian worship in the twenty-first century accommodate the dominant culture, as many contemporary and seeker churches do, incorporating the architecture of sports stadiums and food courts and eliminating symbols like the cross because they are "off-putting" to many people? Or should Christian worship be radically different from the world around it, like the Greek Orthodox or German Amish traditions that separate the worshipper from the dominant culture through both the liturgy and language of worship?

The United Church of Christ includes congregations of many different cultures and countries. Is the cultural context of a local congregation only that of its particular town, ethnic heritage, or nationality, or is it the global

Christian community? Leaders and congregations need to explore such questions of context.

Worship is also *countercultural,* whether it's Joshua telling the tribes to choose amongst the gods that surround them, or Jesus choosing to teach, touch, and eat with women, tax collectors, and other sinners. In our time, simply gathering people together for worship runs counter to our culture's emphasis on individualism and personal spirituality. Likewise, the inclusive invitation to the Communion table counters the climate of fear of "the other," however we define that otherness.

Finally Christian worship is *cross-cultural and intercultural.* It often incorporates different generations in the same community, songs from around the world and across the ages, and prayers not only for the members of that congregation but for God's people of all ages, tongues, and races. Christian worship is cross-cultural and intercultural because in worship, as in the rest of our life together, we seek to follow the way of the One who welcomed Jews and Samaritans, who healed the loved ones of Roman centurions and Jewish leaders, who made room at the table for all kinds of people.

A conscious, concrete, communal, covenantal, and cultural act that seeks to connect us to the eternal power and mystery we call God. To paraphrase the friend on the river trip, another definition of worship could be a structured, intentional, and community-wide beauty attack.

I'd add one more "C" to the adjectives describing worship, and that's *courageous.* Intentionally affirming our faith in God as the source of all life and hope is no small thing in this world. Randall Thompson's "Alleluia" is a good example. He was commissioned to write in the summer of 1940, just after the Nazi invasion of France. It was a fearful time in this country and around the world, yet Thompson chose a word that proclaims our ultimate hope in God: "Alleluia." He explained the "lento" (slow) tempo, saying, "The music in my particular *Alleluia* cannot be made to sound joyous. . . . Here it is comparable to the Book of Job, where it is written, 'The Lord gave and the Lord has taken away. Blessed be the name of the Lord.'"[4]

No matter how softly or slowly, it was a conscious act of courage to sing "Alleluia" in such a fearful and difficult time. Worship is still such an act in our time.

That's the "what" of worship. Let's now turn to the "why."

Three

No Tangible Goods or Services: Why Worship?

"Is being in a boat really so nice as all that?" the Mole asked.
"Nice?" answered the Water Rat. "It's the only thing. . . . Believe me,
my young friend, there is nothing—absolutely nothing—
half so much worth doing as simply messing about in boats . . .
or with boats. . . . In or out of them, it doesn't matter.
Nothing really seems to matter, that's the charm of it."

— Kenneth Grahame, *The Wind in the Willows*[1]

The Water Rat was right. There really is nothing—absolutely nothing—half so much worth doing as simply messing about in boats, especially in the Grand Canyon.

There is also nothing so worthless, at least by the world's standards. The river trip took months of preparation in addition to the three weeks on the river, but it didn't increase the GNP or produce anything of value, other than some great pictures. Nor did the trip enhance our professional lives with CEU's, promotions, or raises.

Adventure, renewal, connection, healing of broken hearts, perspective—

all came from the river. But as the IRS describes charitable donations to the church, "no tangible goods or services were offered in exchange" for the journey.[2]

The same is true of worship. The conscious act of gathering people in the presence of God to express praise and renew their covenant takes time, energy, and usually money. For all that investment, worship is, in Marva Dawn's wonderful description, "a royal waste of time"—at least in earthly terms.[3] Prosperity gospel aside, it offers no promises of job enhancement or success in personal relationships. Unlike Sunday soccer, regular participation in worship won't get your child into a good college.

Scientific studies show that attending church can lower blood pressure, but it can't guarantee a longer life. I've done funerals for faithful church members who came every Sunday, sang in the choir, or ushered, but because of some stupid disease or drunk driver, were cut down in the prime of life. Coming to worship doesn't protect us from sorrow nor from the times we know God's absence more than God's presence.

Then why do it?

Because like a river trip through time and beauty that doesn't increase anyone's productivity or paycheck, worship offers riches beyond imagining. It also compels us for reasons as varied as the people who come to worship.

We Worship Because It's in Our DNA

The philosopher Descartes didn't go far enough in his understanding of what makes us human. Not just "I think, therefore I am," but also "I worship, therefore I am." We human beings have souls, and those souls need to be connected to something bigger than ourselves. We seem to yearn to be lost, if not "in wonder, love, and praise," than in something powerful, sexy, and beyond our control. How else can you explain Rolling Stones concerts, pro-football games, and teenage mosh pits?

I think our need for worship began in the Garden, as soon as the first man and first woman ate the apple and discovered they were ashamed of themselves and afraid of God. We've been trying to reconnect to God and one another ever since, to remind ourselves what life could be like if we actually trusted the One who created us.

We want to remember we were made for that Garden. We want to take off our shoes, not for airport checkpoints, but to stand on sacred ground, in silent awe and in celebration to praise and give thanks to the Source of this whole and holy life. On the river, we got up early to see the first light on the canyon walls and hear the birds waking up. As one person said, "I need a daily infusion of light and song." Worship can offer that.

We Worship Because We Want to Know the True God in the Midst of All the Mini-gods

On the river, there were no ads, pop-ups, or highway billboards. No distractions telling us to buy, eat, or get more. Instead everything pointed to the abundance and mystery of the Creator.

In worship, we use liturgy, music, stories, prayers, and the space itself to do the same. Even if we're worshiping in a storefront, we enter a space deliberately set-aside, sanctified, if only for an hour, to be a place of encounter with the Divine. Different traditions use different architecture and interior arrangements to open us to that encounter. A Greek Orthodox Church filled with icons and candles creates a different world from the simplicity of a clapboard African American chapel in Alabama. But the ornamentation of one and the basic design of the other are both created to remind us *that* we came to worship and *whom* we came to worship.

The world wants us to worship many things—celebrities, cars, clothes. As Reuben Sheares described them, "all the mini-Gods." But on Sunday, he said, "We come to worship the one true God."[4]

We Worship Because We Need Some Way to Practice the Presence of God

God is no more present at 11:00 on a Sunday morning than any other time, nor in a sanctuary more than in a classroom, hospital corridor, or business office. What is different is our *awareness* of that presence. Just as physical exercise helps us train our muscles, worship helps train our souls.

In worship we learn how to focus our attention on what is Eternal. We learn stories of God's interaction with people just like us. We learn how to raise our voices in song and how to "wait upon the Lord" in silence. Most of all, we practice not only believing in God, but *being* the New Creation God calls us to be. We pass God's peace to our brothers and sisters, so we can offer peace in this world. We offer prayers for our world so when we leave, we can care for the world. We practice trusting God's presence in a bit of Communion bread, that we might be able to trust that same presence with the other hungers of our lives.

31

We Worship to Find Our Inner Wholeness

One person took three weeks of unpaid leave to do the river trip. "I needed to get out of this world for a while," she explained, "and go into a deeper world, so I could live more fully and more faithfully in this world."

In her classic *Gift from the Sea*, written fifty years before talk radio and the Internet, Anne Morrow Lindbergh said that in our modern world, the problem we face is "how to remain whole (and) balanced, no matter what centrifugal forces tend to pull one off center."[5]

As a writer, wife, and mother, Lindbergh wrote she often experienced what William James called *Zerrissenheit*—"torn-to-pieces-hood." Echoing the yearnings of many people, then and now, she said:

> I want first of all . . . to be at peace with myself. I want . . .
> a central core to my life that will enable me to carry out these
> obligations and activities as well as I can. I want, in fact—to
> borrow from the language of the saints—to live "in grace" . . .
> to achieve a state of inner spiritual grace from which I could function
> and give as I was meant to in the eye of God.[6]

Many of us come to worship seeking that inner harmony. We turn off our cell phones and iPods and listen instead to ancient texts. We sit in silence and ponder a sermon. And we pray that somewhere in that time, we can find again Lindbergh's central core of "inner spiritual grace."

We Worship to Be Whole People in Body, Soul, and Mind

Perhaps like you, I think—a lot. I also strategize, plan, ponder, perseverate. Consequently, I often forget that God has given me not only a brain, but also ears, eyes, hands, a tongue, and a nose. The river reminded me. Every one of those senses was awake to smell the desert after a rain or gaze in silence at the river's swirls and patterns, to taste the sweet water of a canyon stream or feel the warm earth beneath my feet. Sand in my sheets and a few insect bites were a small price to pay for three weeks of being a whole human being.

Worship is also a sensual affair that invites us to experience our lives; in the words of e.e. cummings, as the "tasting touching hearing seeing breathing" human beings we are created to be.[7] Some Christian traditions know that more than others, as my incense- and pageantry-loving Roman Catholic friends remind me. But even the most staid New England church has its own unique smells of candle wax and musty hymnals, the creak of wooden floors, and the taste of Welch's in a communion glass.

In her novel *Beloved,* Toni Morrison tells how the "unchurched preacher" Baby Suggs called the former slaves of her community to worship. Gathering them in a forest clearing, she first told the children to laugh, the men to dance, and the women to cry. Then she mixed it all up until, "exhausted and riven," they fell into the damp grass and she "offered up to them her great big heart."

> "Here," she said, "in this here place, we flesh; flesh that weeps, laughs; flesh that dances on bare feet in the grass. Love it. Love it hard. Yonder they do not love your flesh. They despise it. . . . *You* got to love it, *you!* . . . This is flesh I'm talking about here. Flesh that needs to be loved."[8]

Then, Morrison, concludes, Baby Suggs stood and "danced with her twisted hip what her heart had to say."[9]

The sensuality of worship reminds us not only that God came to us in the flesh, the Incarnation, but also that God loves us in *our* incarnation, *our* flesh.

We Worship Because It Challenges Us to Be More than We Think We Can Be

The rapids of the Colorado River are the biggest and longest in the country. Other U.S. rapids are rated on a scale of 1 to 5. The Colorado's go all the way to 10. You can hear the sound of some of them from the rim of the canyon, a mile above. Just being a passenger in a raft, much less rowing the whole river, requires chutzpah one doesn't normally need or use.

But that challenge is a reason for the journey. If there's no greater fear than scouting a #10 rapid like Crystal, with its huge holes and never-ending hydraulics, there's also no greater feeling than to be able to say on the other side, "We did it!"

Worship also challenges us to get to the other side of our fear and doubt. We live in a world that can sometimes seem as scary as any Colorado rapid. But in worship, we're called to love this world as passionately as God loves it. Sometimes, we come through the sanctuary doors as fearful of failure or rejection as the most novice river runner fears Lava Falls. But worship tells us we are beloved of God and demands that we claim that inheritance.

33

In worship we hear Isaiah and Jesus proclaim "the Spirit of the Lord is upon me," and we pray that same Spirit be upon us so we can do what they did. We sing of God's reign of justice and peace, and pray that the God of grace and glory will give us the wisdom and courage to bring it forth in our lives and in this world.

We Worship Because It Puts Life in Perspective

Floating through 1.7-billion-year-old rock is a good reminder of our place in the universe. You can almost hear God's voice from the whirlwind of Job: "Where were you when I laid the foundation of the earth . . . when the morning stars together and all the heavenly beings shouted for joy?" (Job 38: 4, 7).

In worship, we hear questions like that. We also hear stories from that great cloud of witnesses whose faith and courage far exceeds our own, or at least mine. In worship, we break bread and share the cup to remember that God's best is more powerful than our worst.

Evelyn Underhill writes of worship that "it points steadily toward the reality of God: gives, expresses, and maintains that which is the essence of all sane religion—a theocentric basis to life."[10] In a culture whose motto is "have it your way," worship proclaims a God whose ways are not our own but who is "the way, the truth, and the life" (John 14:6).

In Christian worship, we use prayers of confession and songs of praise to get life back into perspective. In Navajo sacred traditions, the Blessingway, a multiday "Sing," does the same. Barney Mitchell, a Navajo Singer explains:

> The Blessingway is like an "engine tune-up." It is prescribed, when a man or woman is not "tuned to what's around him"—he's not tuned to what he's about, what he encounters. He feels exaggerated. . . . The Blessingway is so you won't feel exaggerated.[11]

A paradox of worship is that even as it keeps us from feeling exaggerated, it also reminds us of our status as children of a loving God. "Take, eat," says the pastor at Communion. "This bread is broken for *you*." No matter what the world says about our value and worth, worship tells us and shows us how beloved we are. It invites us to trust there is One who hears both our songs of praise and our sighs too deep for words. It also invites us to trust that our friends and neighbors in the worshipping community will listen and hear as well.

"I go to church," a member said, "to be reminded who created the heavens and the earth." "Church is the place I go," wrote a young confirmand, "when the world has forgotten my name."[12] We need both perspectives to know our place in the universe. Worship can offer both.

We Worship Because We Need to Receive Blessing

The coolness of a canyon morning. A cup of coffee left by my tent the day I overslept. The surprise of a waterfall after a long hike down a slot canyon. Time and again, the river, the canyon, and the community of friends bestowed blessings, large and small.

Worship does the same. There is the sacramental blessing of baptism or the sacred blessing of a wedding or covenant service. We ask God's blessing "of Word and Spirit" on the elements of Communion and on all of us who share the meal. When first graders receive their "God Loves Me" Bibles and eighth graders get their NRSVs, they and their parents receive the laying on of hands. Even their new Bibles are blessed by the prayers of the congregation.

Worship also blesses us in less formal ways. The "sweet, sweet spirit" of music that takes our minds off whatever is troubling us and reconnects us to beauty and grace, if only for a moment. The chance just to sit in the sanctuary and watch the light stream though windows. The laughter of children and the touch of another's hand in the passing of the peace.

"It is only framed in space that beauty blooms," wrote Anne Morrow Lindbergh. "A tree has significance if one sees it against the empty face of sky. A note in music gains significance from the silences on either side."[13] The structure, rhythm, and space of worship frame our lives so we can receive God's blessings and so that beauty can bloom in our souls and in this world.

We Worship Because We Also Need to Bestow Blessing

It's a basic need—not just to receive but to offer blessing. Worship provides tangible ways to do that in the morning offering or the passing of the peace. Our choir director reminds her singers they are not just performing but blessing the congregation with the gift of God's presence through their music.

Sometimes simply showing up for worship bestows blessing. We never know who might need our voice to sing when they haven't got a song, our silent prayers to remind them they're not alone, our hand to offer them a sign of peace when their hearts or their families are troubled. In short, we never know who might need to be blessed by our presence as an incarnation of God's presence.

We Worship Because We Need to Enjoy
This World and the One Who Made It

We played a lot on the river—water fights, paco pad relays, dress-up nights. We traded jokes and invented "fifty things you can do with a Yard 'o Beef" (don't ask). We all had highly responsible jobs back home, but the river time was playtime.

The world can be a very serious place. Coming into the presence of God can be very serious business. Our worship needs to take both seriously, whether by evoking an awareness of God's awesomeness, as Isaiah experienced in the temple, or by lifting up the cares of the world, as echoed in his cry of woe for himself and his people.

But according to the Bible, God also created great whales, "just for the sport of it"; a garden called Eden, which sounds like "enjoyment" in Hebrew; and male and female because that first earth being was lonely. We're created in that same playful divine image. Worship calls us to remember that.

Pueblo and Hopi peoples include mudheads, sacred clowns, and other "delight makers" in their dances and rituals. "Too much power, too much seriousness," states a study of Native American traditions, "were to be feared for they too could 'unbalance' life in the community and the environment. We are taught by the clowns . . . not to make ourselves too important. We are not that *indispensable*."[14]

Making oneself a mudhead for Christ is equally important in Christian worship.

We Worship Because We Need "Some Kind of Tomorrow"

Every day was a new day on the river, offering new places to explore and new stories to tell about the river and ourselves.

Of course, every day is a new day anywhere. As Frederick Buechner writes, "Using the same old materials of earth, air, fire, and water, every twenty-four hours, God creates something new out of them. . . . Every morning you wake up to something that in all eternity never was before and never will be again. And the you that wakes up was never the same before and will never be the same again either."[15]

Worship wakes us up to that newness. We sing, "Morning has broken, like the first morning." We get trumpets to play "Christ the Lord Is Risen Today" on Easter, use candles on Christmas Eve to remember the light born in the dead of winter, and adorn the sanctuary in red on Pentecost to celebrate the birth of the Christian church.

We hear stories about people who got new names: Abram to Abraham; Peter the Denier to Peter the Leader; Saul to Paul. We learn of others who came to dead-ends and found new life: an unwed peasant girl who became the mother of God; a multimarried Samaritan woman who recognized the Messiah; a woman with seven demons who became the first witness to the resurrection.

We participate in rituals, some of them ancient, that also celebrate new life. We lay hands on our first graders before they head off for the first day of school. We initiate our youth as they leave their childhood and start their journey to adulthood. We bless couples as they begin a new stage of life and commitment together.

Sunday itself is the day Christ conquered death and brought new life. We can come to worship defeated by this world, deadened by its sorrows and hurts, and somehow in that time of gathering with others for praise and prayer, something in us changes and we come back to life.

Tom was an elderly gentleman in a congregation I once served. A retired professor of physics, he was nationally known for his research. He'd always gone to church, because that's what his generation did, but his real excitement came in scientific discovery.

When his wife of forty-seven years died, Tom felt completely lost. Life didn't seem worth living without his beloved Elsie. He hardly went out of the house except on Sundays. And doing that saved his life, he said. Not because of any specific thing the preacher said, not even because of the care of the community. "Going to worship was important," he said. "It's what got me out of bed on Sunday mornings."

Still it wasn't enough. Then one Sunday morning, when he had just about given up, Tom sat holding his little glass of grape juice during Communion. Waiting until everyone was served, he noticed how the pulse in his wrist moved the glass ever so slightly. He kept watching that tiny movement every time his heart beat. In that moment, he said, "I realized I was still alive and that it was *good* to be alive, there in that beautiful space, with that wonderful music, and all those good people. For the first time in a long time, I looked forward to my life."

Toni Morrison in *Beloved* tells of Paul D, a former slave whose neck still bears the mark of a slave collar, and Sethe, the woman he loves. "Sethe," he says one night, "me and you, we got more yesterday than anybody. We need some kind of tomorrow."[16]

In our world and our personal lives, we need some kind of tomorrow.

Worship, offering "no tangible goods or services," but simply gathering us in the presence of God and in community with others, can give us that gift beyond measure.

That's why we worship.

Four

Sacred Rhythm:
Structure and Elements

Before talking of holy things, we prepare ourselves by offerings....
One will fill his pipe and hand it to the other who will light it and offer
it to the sky and earth.... They will smoke together...
then they will be ready to talk.

—Mato-Kuwapi, or Chased-by-Bears, a Santee-Yanktonai Sioux[1]

On the river, every day was different: new canyons to explore, new rapids to scout and run. But every day also had the same rhythm and rituals. Get up at first light, stuff your sleeping bag, and fold your tent before the first cup of coffee. Help with breakfast. Load the boats. Explore the next section of the river. Find a campsite, unload, set up, fix dinner, sleep, and get up the next day to do it all again. Every day was different, but the rituals and rhythms allowed us to experience whatever the river and the canyon had to offer that day.

The same is true of Christian worship, regardless of the tradition or denomination. Megachurch or Mennonite, Greek Orthodox or Tahitian Congregational, church camp vespers or a high Catholic mass, all worship has a basic rhythm and structure that lead us into the encounter with the living God and then back out into the world. The particular symbols, music, "stage direction," and props may differ, but the flow remains the same:

- Gather the people.
- Help them prepare their hearts, souls, and minds.
- Engage them in the lively and transforming Word of God.
- Invite their response.
- Send them into the world as a new creation.

Sunday morning Communion or a Saturday night wedding, if it's worship, the structure has a purpose: Get people together in sacred space and sacred time, get them connected to God's Word and in God's presence, give them ways to respond, and get them out of there and back into the world, transformed and empowered, be it for the next week or the rest of their lives.

Gather the People

Gather Them in a Sacred Space and Sacred Time
The Orthodox and Catholics probably do this part better than most. When you step through the doors of their churches, you know you are entering a different world than the one you left behind. It looks different, with icons or santos, altar rails and ambos. It sounds different, often hushed and quiet. It even smells different, with a whiff of the incense used at the service just before.

But even in our spare Reformed Protestant tradition, we use verbal and visual "cues" that tell the congregation we are stepping onto holy ground, in holy time. The plainness of many of our sanctuaries stands in contrast to the outside world of ads and brand names plastered on buses and baseball fields. Whether the music we hear is Palestrina or praise music, it also reminds us that we have come to do something different than what we do in our everyday lives. Even without incense, the smell of candle wax, flowers, and mustiness can be a sacred reminder of where we are.

Gather Them in Praise of God
"There's only one thing you need to know about God," goes the oft-told story about the AA sponsor talking to his new sponsee agonizing over the Higher Power language. "You ain't it."

Worship begins in praise to remind us "we ain't it." Most of us come to worship from a culture that wants us to believe that we and our children are the most important thing in the world and that the world (and its resources) needs to be organized around our desires. From the opening of worship, help your congregation remember who truly "is It."

There are lots of ways to do that. For Isaiah, the seraphim flew around God's throne singing "Holy, Holy, Holy." At the United Church, we begin slightly less dramatically with a simple "Alleluia" or the Taizé song "Laudate Omnes Gentes" ("Sing Praises, All You People"). Other congregations begin worship fifteen minutes before the hour with several "praise songs" that help warm up and open up the congregation to God's Spirit.

Even if your congregation likes to have announcements and prayer requests shared at the beginning of the service (before the call to worship or opening hymn), take time to gather the people in praise before turning to the business of the church. Let them know from the start why you're there. Praise God.

Let God's praise echo in the call to worship and opening hymn. The first few moments set the stage for the rest of the service. But don't limit that praise only to the beginning. Praise God throughout the service, after the prayer of invocation or confession, in the pastoral prayer, as you bless the offering, and as you send people out into the world. If a fundamental purpose of worship is to turn our attention back to God, then praising God should be both the Alpha and the Omega of any service.

Gather Them with Blessing

In that sacred space and time, remind the congregation that *they* are a sacred people, a blessed people. Paul began with blessing. "Grace and peace to you," he wrote in every letter to new Christians (except the Galatians, of course). Grace and peace to you called to be saints—even if you're not feeling very saintly that morning.

"The love of God, the light of Christ, and the power and communion of the Holy Spirit" is one way to offer that blessing. So is a song like "Sweet, Sweet Spirit" or a paraphrase of Psalm 100 ("Come into God's presence with singing, for it is God who made us and we are God's"). Such blessings acknowledge what we're looking for in that hour, even if we don't have the words to say it ourselves.

Begin with the blessing, because perhaps if that's the first word we hear we might be able to hear harder words later on.

Jesus knew that. So did the early church. Why else would the collective memory of the Sermon on the Mount begin with the Beatitudes? It's no accident that the first words out of Jesus' mouth in worship, as the church remembered them, were "Blessed are you."

That "you" encompassed everyone there—the poor in spirit and the poor in goods; the ones in mourning and the ones trying to make peace; the passionate ones working for justice and righteousness and even the bored ones there because they didn't have any better place to go or anything better to do.

Only after that blessing did Jesus start to tell them what else they needed to hear—the teachings about turning the other cheek, going the extra mile, and the other ways he called them to discipleship. But before those difficult words, he started with a word of blessing because what they needed to hear first and foremost was that they were blessed from the top of their heads to the soles of their feet, blessed in the words of the Navajo Beautyway, "above, below, behind, in front, all around."[2]

To gather the people in blessing is not just to make them feel good nor does it contradict my earlier encouragement to gather the people in the praise of God. Indeed, one could argue gathering in blessing is the most radical thing we do in worship. Being reminded that we are blessed by God runs counter to our consumer culture of insatiable desires. In contrast, God's blessing is not something we can buy or even earn. It is both freely bestowed and ever abundant. That's a radical message in our world of shopping malls and hedge funds.

Two, to gather the people in blessing is to remind them of their true identity. Rev. Yvonne Delk, the first African American woman ordained in the UCC, tells of her parents, who six days a week worked in a world that regarded them as nobody. But on Sunday, they dressed in their finest, went to church where they were greeted as "Brother" and "Sister," and reminded from the beginning that they were beloved children of God. When they stepped through the church doors, they stepped into their true home, a holy place where their holiness was affirmed and blessing was bestowed.[3]

Three, to gather the people in blessing is to empower them to bless others. Perhaps if, as Fred Craddock often encourages, we "begin with the benediction,"[4] then the people in our congregations might be better able to see the person next to them as also blessed, or the person in front of them or the people you're going to ask them to pray for, those Iraqis and Islamists, the hungry and homeless. Later in prayer we may ask our congregations to bless this whole difficult world, and few of us (the preacher included) can offer a true blessing unless we know how deeply *we* ourselves are blessed.

You can always repeat it at the end of the service, but "begin with the benediction." Gather them in blessing. God knows they need it, and so do we who are leading worship.

Gather the Joys, Thanksgivings, and Concerns of the Congregation

Part of the heritage of the United Church of Christ is the Congregational Meetinghouse where the church was the center of community life. In many congregations, that tradition continues in the sharing of announcements and prayer concerns. At United, we do so early in the service so as to not interrupt the flow of worship. As we've grown, we've had to limit announcements, which not everyone likes. One parishioner told me that the announcements, especially of political gatherings, were her favorite part of worship. (She was a former Unitarian.) Given the hectic nature of the world outside the sanctuary, I err on the side of incorporating more music, silence, and prayer and fewer announcements.

We share prayer requests, be they for healing a broken heart, a broken bone, or a broken world. As the congregation has grown, we now encourage people to call or e-mail the church by Sunday morning with their concerns so the worship leader can incorporate them.

Make sure to balance the "concerns" with the "joys and thanksgivings"— births, adoptions, new jobs, promotions, or the fact it rained. We need to remind ourselves that God is a God of life and new possibilities, as well as being a God who holds us and our world in the hard times.

Gather with the Breath of God

"Breathing in God's Gifts" is a ritual that we use not only in worship, but also in council and other meetings. After the announcements and prayer concerns, the worship leader asks the congregation, "Let us breathe in the gift of God's peace." We pause and breathe. Then "Let us breathe in the gift of God's hope." Then "And let us breathe in the gift of God's love."

After breathing together, we stand and offer those gifts to one another in the passing of the peace. A verse or two of a familiar hymn brings us back together. Then before going deeper into worship, we breathe in God's gifts once again.

This "ritual of breathing" began years ago for purely practical reasons. There was no door between the tiny narthex and the sanctuary, so conversations and other noise carried into the beginning of the service. Breathing together signaled the start of the service and helped people get settled.

Over the years, the ritual has taken on deeper meaning. Breathing in God's gifts reminds us of the source of our lives and what God offers us in those lives. It also acknowledges the sense of exhaustion and anxiety that many people bring to worship. Breathing together helps us focus and fills us, individually and as a congregation, with God's sweet and powerful Spirit.

Praise, blessing, breathing. Once we've gathered with that, the liturgist stands at the pulpit, invites the congregation into the "formal" call to worship, and we sing the opening hymn.

This may sound like a lot to do at the beginning of a service, but it only takes a few minutes. In a world of so many distractions and concerns, taking time to help people catch their breath (literally), turn their attention to God, and begin to trust they are blessed is, I believe, time well spent.

Help Them Prepare Their Hearts, Souls, and Minds

Technically this could go under the previous section, at least in the traditional four-fold structure of worship (gathering, Word, Eucharist, sending). But I think "preparing" to receive the Word deserves attention.

Some congregations do that preparation in a prayer of invocation, putting into words what, at United, we do through breathing together—i.e., opening up and letting God in. Whatever our specific prayer, in the invocation we say both, in the words of one hymn, "Here I am, Lord," and in the words of another, "Fill me, Lord."

Other congregations combine the invocation with a prayer of confession. To take in God's Spirit and Word, we often have to let go of certain things, like anger or selfishness. To put it in the vernacular, we have to confess stuff— turn it over, give it up, expose it, say "Here God, here's what I've done or what we've done. I know it wasn't right, I am truly sorry, and I pray that you will forgive me/us so I/we can move ahead in this relationship with you."

Okay, there are more formal ways of saying all that, such as "Forgive us for the harm we have done and the good we have left undone." But the gist is the same.

But, I confess, it makes me very nervous to use words like "confession" or include a prayer of confession in worship. I don't want the congregation to tune out before we hardly get started. I also know that on any given Sunday, there are people in the congregation who come from traditions where words like sin, repentance, and confession were used to denigrate and shame, *not* free and empower.

44

As a young minister, I mightily resisted imposing confession on a congregation for the same reason Paul told the Corinthians he wouldn't eat food sacrificed to idols. He knew such food didn't have any negative consequences, but he also knew that his eating it could cause a brother or sister to stumble. Therefore he would abstain. I did the same with prayers of confession.

An opportunity to get out of my own cultural and religious skin helped me understand confession in a new way. On a brief sabbatical years ago, I lived with a Navajo family outside of Canyon de Chelly to learn about Native American spirituality and understandings. Along with soaking in the landscape, I participated in Blessingways and other "Sings," especially for healing.

In such ceremonies in native sacred traditions, Beck and Walters write in *The Sacred*:

> Certain procedures are followed in order to prepare the mind and the body to be *receptive*, to be aware. [The first is] *Purifying*. Now you erase your thoughts. You get rid of all poisons and excesses in your body through sweat baths, emetics (herbal drinks to make a person vomit), bathing, smoking, and smudging (blowing smoke of cedar, sage, or sweetgrass for example, on the body). You make yourself empty.[5]

That was born out in the first Blessingway I experienced. The participant (an uncle in the family) had to purify himself at the beginning of the "Sing" so its words and power could come into his soul. In that moment, I finally realized what a prayer of confession is about—i.e., letting go of whatever keeps us from God, so we can let in God's healing and power and get back in harmony with God, the world, and ourselves.

I wouldn't ask a congregation to purify to quite the extent of a native tradition, but I do believe it's important to empty ourselves of the greed, fears, and selfishness that are toxic not only to us but to others. When we have hurt someone, we can't have an honest conversation, much less a loving relationship, until we've acknowledged what we've done. We need to do the same in our relationship with God.

The content of the prayer may differ, depending on the context of the congregation. We may need to confess our abuse of power, personally or socially. We may need to confess our fear of *using* the power God has given us. We may need to ask forgiveness for the ways we've hurt our families or circles of friends. We may also need to confess our failure to care for the whole human family or for the earth.

Jeffery Rowthorn suggests that prayers of confession can be sung as well as spoken. In our war-torn time, the third verse of "God of Grace and God of Glory" could be printed in the bulletin or sung by the choir, either with a spoken prayer or alone:

> Cure your children's warring madness,
> bend our lives to your control.
> Shame our wanton selfish gladness,
> rich in things but poor in soul.

Follow it with a time of silent prayer, then invite the congregation or choir to sing:

> Grant us wisdom, grant us courage,
> Make our broken spirits whole,
> Make our broken spirits whole.[6]

Other musical prayers of confession could include "O God, How We Have Wandered" (Passion Chorale); "Sweet Little Jesus Boy"; or "Just as I Am."

A caveat: If you lead people into a time of confession, make sure you *lead them out of it*. Often, especially in our justice-conscious UCC, we fall into what William Sloane Coffin described as the greatest sin of all, "believing there is more sin in us than grace in God." Yes, we have all sinned and fallen short, be it as a nation or as individuals, but we also believe in a God whose reach is very long.

Whether your congregation calls it "The Assurance of Pardon," "The Affirmation of God's Grace," or another name for God's forgiveness and love, offer it with the same authority you used to call them into confession—which means you need to believe in that grace and pardon as much for yourself as for the congregation. Then sing God's praise and your thanks once again.

Engage Them in the Lively and Transforming Word of God

Historically the Protestant tradition has focused on the hearing, interpreting, understanding, and acting upon the Word of God. For the United Church of Christ, that has been a powerful Word. It moved the early Pilgrims and German immigrants to leave a known world for a new one. Seeking to be faithful to that Word, some Congregational Abolitionists took up the case of the Amistad Africans and others moved to "Kansas, bloody Kansas" to bring it into the Union as a free state.

God's Word inspired Connecticut Yankees to sail halfway around the world as Christian missionaries to Hawaii. A century and a half later, that same Word motivated their heirs to confess the harm done to native Hawaiians in the name of Christ.

In the 1950s and '60s, the liberating Word of God gave young African Americans the courage to move to the front of the bus. And it has given the UCC the courage to march for the rights of farm workers and to advocate for gay and lesbian persons long before other Christian denominations.

The Word of God has indeed been powerful in our church. Our worship needs to engage people as fully as possible in it.

The chapter on "The Word as Sacrament" outlines the central role of preaching in vital worship, why it's important, and how to think about it in terms of planning, content, and delivery.

Here, I would like to offer some additional ways to engage the Word. Without negating the importance of preaching, our worship can also include opportunities to experience God's Word in other forms and in voices other than the preacher's.

Before offering those examples, however, a word about the lectionary. Should we follow it every Sunday? For me, the answer is yes and no. In planning a season of worship, I review all four lessons for each Sunday. It's a good discipline and keeps me connected to the wider church. It can also keep me from riding (or beating) the same horse every Sunday.

However, there are times when what's happening in the world or in the life of the church calls for a particular word other than the word from the lectionary Scriptures. I am glad to be part of the "free church" tradition that links us to the wider Christian communion through the lectionary, but also give us the freedom to follow God's Spirit and our own instincts.

So what are some ways, in addition to preaching, of engaging that word? Some possibilities:

"How Did You Experience the Presence of God?"

That's a question I ask the congregation in a variety of settings: council meetings, retreats, youth groups. It can also be used in worship. For Labor Day, ask three persons in different lines of work to reflect on their experience of God's presence (or absence) in their jobs. If your church has particular outreach

47

ministries, such as serving meals at a homeless shelter or tutoring children at a local school, invite a volunteer from those ministries to share how and where they saw the face of God in the service of others. When the youth return from their mission trip, ask them the same question and build Sunday worship around their answers.

The Music Is the Message

Many churches will devote a Sunday to the offering of a large sacred work, such as Antonio Vivaldi's *Gloria* or Ariel Ramirez's *Nuestra Navidad* (the story of the Flight to Egypt). At United, we've adopted Moravian "Singstude" services, where the message is offered solely through hymns. The music director or minister could choose them, or ask four people in the congregation of different ages and backgrounds to talk about a song that gives them hope or speaks to them of God. If it's not in the hymnal (and for anyone under forty, it probably won't be) find a way for the congregation, or at least the choir to sing it.

Voices from the Community

In the UCC, we affirm "God is still speaking," including through people of other faiths and vocations outside the Christian church. One Palm Sunday, I invited the local rabbi to do a "dialogue sermon" with me on "What Christians Can Learn from Jews, and What Jews Can Learn from Christians." His answers definitely made us think in new ways about Holy Week.

Another time, when the Santa Fe Symphony and Chorus was performing Beethoven's Ninth Symphony, their conductor, Steven Smith, and I shared a "sacred conversation" on worship, focused on the "new song" of Psalm 96 and Beethoven's masterpiece. He noted that at a time when the relationships between Christians and Muslims mirrored our own, Beethoven included a Turkish march in his most famous work, underscoring music's power to unite the human community, then and now.[7]

Variations on a Traditional Theme

Thanksgiving is a good example. The Scripture lessons from Deuteronomy or the Psalms tell us to bring to worship the "first fruits of the harvest." In the UCC, the holiday can evoke images of English Pilgrims and Native Americans sharing those "first fruits" at the first Thanksgiving feast

Perhaps for you as for me, none of the four parishes I've served ever had a preponderance of farmers. Yet all of us have been given gifts from God to offer in thanksgiving and for the common good. As a student intern in Tempe, Arizona, I wanted our "harvest" to be in our setting of a twentieth-century Southwest suburb, not a seventeenth-century New England colony. I asked three members to think of a "gift they had been given for the common good" and a symbol for it. In place of the sermon, each person spoke of their particular talent or skill and then put their symbol on the altar. A retired attorney brought a clock to represent the gift of time he had to volunteer in ways he couldn't when he was working. A teacher used pens and paper to symbolize her ability to help children read and write. A bookkeeper for a small business placed his ledger on the altar and gave thanks for the ability to keep the company solvent and the workers employed.

We still sang "We Gather Together" and "Come Ye, Thankful People, Come," but the service helped expand our understanding of God's harvest and what we were thankful for.

Epiphany (or "Three Kings Day") is another sacred day with a set story that can be made new. Ask three people to study Matthew's story of the Magi and think about stars they've followed, times they've gotten lost in Herod's court, or found themselves in unlikely places (like a barn in Bethlehem) where they've seen Christ. On Epiphany Sunday, invite them to be the Wise Ones.

Once you start to engage the congregation with God's Word, all kinds of possibilities come to mind. Don't overdo it, of course—offer such services five or six times year at the most. Also, these suggestions aren't meant to detract from the central role of preaching in worship nor are they an excuse for the preacher not doing his or her homework.

But don't be afraid to try new ways, along with the sermon, to open up the Word of God to the congregation. Help people get inside that Word so that it can get inside them and transform them.

However the Word is offered, give the congregation silent time afterward to reflect on what they've heard. In Native American vision quests, such silence is "a time for the individual to think about the things that made him or her strong and . . . be open to the possibility that some spirit might come to him/her in this time."[8] Make sure your worship also offers time for the Spirit to do its work.

Invite Their Response

As Christians, we believe in the "Incarnation," which simply means God's Word became flesh (*carne* in Latin) in Jesus Christ. We also believe that we are called to make that word flesh in our lives and in the life of our world.

Therefore, we don't just receive the Word. We also respond to it with our prayers and our offerings.

Offering Ourselves in Prayer

"I have two main objections to the pastoral prayers I hear," wrote Will Willimon. "They are not prayers and they are not pastoral." Willimon agreed with Leander Keck, former dean of Yale Divinity School, who characterized the pastoral prayer as "a bowl of wet, soggy noodles dumped on a helpless congregation."[9]

Our more liturgical brothers and sisters can rely on their *Book of Common Prayer* or missalettes for their pastoral prayer or prayers of the people. We in the "free church" tradition generally have to make them up ourselves. We need to make sure they are not "wet soggy noodles," but instead both prayerful and pastoral.

Let's start with what the pastoral prayer is not, namely it's not a "sermonette." It's not a second chance for the pastor to say what she didn't get a chance to say in the sermon, nor is it the opportunity for another worship leader to say what he *wished* the pastor had said.

The pastoral prayer is a prayer, meaning its focus is God, not the parishioner we're afraid might have missed the point of the sermon nor the preacher we think lacks the courage of our convictions. I heard a story once about President Lyndon Johnson asking Bill Moyers, his then press secretary, to say the blessing at a state dinner. Moyers began the prayer, but Johnson quickly interrupted him. "Speak up, Bill! I can't hear you." Moyers replied, "I wasn't speaking to you, sir."

That's also true of the pastoral prayer. Unlike the sermon that speaks to the people, the prayer speaks to God. Like the rest of worship, it speaks of our thanks, our praise, our hopes, sometimes our doubts or our need for healing. It also speaks of our desire to do God's will and to respond with our lives to the Word we have heard, the blessings we remember, and the challenges we face in our faith.

Like the "our" of the Lord's Prayer (also known as The Prayer of Our Savior), the "our" of the pastoral prayer moves us beyond the individual petitions or needs we bring to worship. Instead we are invited to pray for one another in the church community, remembering that, in the apostle Paul's words, "if one member suffers, all suffer together with it; if one member is honored, all rejoice together with it." (I Corinthians 12:26) It also moves us beyond the walls of our particular church community to offer prayers for "all God's children" as the African American spiritual declares or "all our relations" as Native Americans pray.

Because the pastoral prayer seeks to embrace the wider human community, it can easily become what Willimon describes as "abstract, nonspecific, detached, formalized ramblings that sound as if they were prayed by one who is a stranger to the congregation."[10] Like the sermon, the pastoral prayer must be deeply rooted in the life of the community. Whether in prayer or in sermon, our authority on Sunday morning comes in large part from our leadership and pastoral listening the other six days of the week.

By no means is the pastor the only one capable or authorized to offer the pastoral prayer. In many congregations, it's the responsibility of a Deacon or other lay leader. Jeffery Rowthorn suggests a "pastoral prayer preparation group" as a way to shape the prayer that comes from the life of the congregation.[11] Gather an intentional group and ask questions such as: "How does the Scripture lesson inform the prayer of the day? What prayers are needed by the congregation or wider world? What are the prayers of thanks do we have to offer?" Members of the group could take responsibility on a rotating basis for composing and even offering the prayer. Even if the pastoral prayer is seen as the pastor's responsibility, such a group can enrich its content.

We speak to God in the pastoral prayers. It's also a time to let God speak to us. Silence, as much as spoken word, is a part of the prayer. Silence can come at the end, before the Lord's Prayer, or be woven into the prayer itself. For example, if the pastoral prayer begins with thanks and praise, lead into a time of silent prayer with "Help us now in silent prayer to remember the ways each of us have known your grace and love." If the pastoral prayer includes prayers for peace in the world, ask God to "help us listen for the ways you call each of us to be peacemakers, in our lives and in our world."

In some congregations, the pastoral prayer leads into intercessory prayers offered by individuals in the congregation. It's a long-standing tradition at United, but I admit to mixed feelings about it. On the plus side, intercessory prayer allows for the movement of God's Spirit in the life of the congregation. It can empower the congregation and engage the faith and vision of the community beyond that of the worship leaders.

It can also open a can of worms. On the minus side, intercessory prayer is sometimes used to make political statements, preach the sermon the intercessor wanted the minister to give, or be used as therapy for the person praying. Spoken intercessions can also interrupt the silence that others value. On a purely practical level, as a congregation or sanctuary gets bigger, it becomes harder to hear prayers that aren't amplified.

Like the rest of worship, no one way fits every church. But pay attention to the pastoral prayer. See if the way you're doing it still fits the congregation as it is now. Most of all, regardless of how you shape it or offer it, make sure the pastoral prayer does what all good prayer (and worship) does—gives thanks to God, lets God into our lives, and feeds God's people with the solid food of faith. No wet, soggy noodles on the menu.

Offering Our Gifts in Thanksgiving.
If you love someone, you want to do something for them. In fact, if you really love them, you'd do anything for them. Ask any parent.

In worship, the offering comes after the sermon and the pastoral prayer, both of which remind us of God's love and grace in our lives. The offering is a chance to give something back to the Source of that love and grace.

The Bible is filled with all kinds of ways people sought to give God what they thought God wanted—turtle doves, bulls, fatted calves, first fruits of the harvest. Such offerings sometimes added extra dimensions to worship, like the time Abraham sacrificed various animals and then spent the night scaring the vultures away from the altar. Then there was the time he thought God wanted his son to be the morning offering. We should probably be glad our churches only take cash or checks.

Of course, we can't truly give anything to the One who is the Maker of Everything. But we can give something to the ones that Creator cares about.

That's part of love as well. If we truly love someone, then we also love the people they love. In the case of God, that includes everybody, from our brothers and sisters in the church community to our friends and neighbors in the rest of the world.

The offering is one way to make that love incarnate. That's why presenting our offering is an act of worship and not just a drop in the box on the way out, depending on how much we liked the sermon.

Singing praise to God "from whom all blessings flow" may seem like an odd thing to do after we've sacrificed some of our hard-earned money. Maybe it would help to remember what it felt like the first time you fell in love and had your first chance to give your beloved something that showed them the breadth of that love. Your heart may well have sung a bit even as you handed over your precious gift. Consider the doxology that kind of love song.

Send Them into the World as a New Creation

You've gathered them, prepared them, given them the Word, and offered a chance to respond. Hopefully, you've also given them your best. Now get them out of there. If as leaders and congregation, you've done your job, the world needs what you've been given and what you've become in that hour.

Choose a closing hymn that combines praise of God with commissioning of the people. Similarly, let your benediction blend commissioning with blessing. The commissioning part constitutes the congregation's "marching orders" to be the new creation. The blessing part reminds them who they are, Who goes with them into the world, and Who will call them back to worship once again.

Derived from two Latin words—*bene* meaning "well" and *dicere* meaning "to speak"—a benediction is a time we "speak well," giving the congregation final words of encouragement and boldness. It is also a time when we, as worship leaders, make incarnate those bold words of blessing. Give the congregation some tangible sign of that blessing: raise one hand, make the sign of the cross, hold up both arms. You're sending people into a world often filled with fear, hatred, and uncertainty. Let your last words, and actions, dedicate the congregation to God's care and keeping. Speak your benediction well to give them the courage and hope they need to trust God and love God's people in such a world.

Gather. Prepare. Engage. Respond. Send. Whether on Sunday morning or Christmas Eve, in a cathedral sanctuary or by a hospital bed, that's the rhythm of worship, the ritual of life.

Five

A Pilgrimage in Time: The Year in Worship

Return to the deep sources, nothing less
Will nourish the torn spirit, the bewildered heart,
The angry mind: and from the ultimate duress
Pierced with the breath of anguish, speak for love.

Return, return to the deep sources, nothing less
Will teach the stiff hands a new way to serve,
To carve into our lives the forms of tenderness
And still that ancient, necessary pain preserve . . .

—May Sarton[1]

I had never run the Colorado River, but I have been in and around the Grand Canyon since I was a toddler and my mother had to keep her insatiably curious three-year-old from venturing over the edge. When I was twelve, we drove in an old Ford station wagon through two hundred miles of desert on dirt road to get to the North Rim. I still remember the sweet smell of the river at Lee's Ferry.

I was twenty-two when I, along with my sister, hiked into the Inner

55

Gorge down to the river while my mother and a friend rode the mules down. It was in December, and our packs were heavy in those pre-Gortex days. We slid on the ice the first two miles.

I visited the Canyon over the next twenty-five years, but didn't hike down again until the summer of 2000. I was camping on the North Rim, and was able to get a last-minute reservation at the bottom. I headed out before dawn. Fourteen miles later, I'd made it to the river. It was 115 degrees. That evening, I called my mother from the outdoor phone to tell her where I was and thank her for that first trip twenty-five years before.

I also called because she was in the middle of chemotherapy for a cancer that had metastasized earlier that summer. In typical fashion, she didn't let on much, but I knew something was wrong. That night I lay outside on a picnic table, looking at the stars, and letting myself be held by billion-year-old rock. The next day I hiked up to the South Rim and drove to Phoenix instead of back to Santa Fe.

Three years later, during Lent, I again hiked down to the river, walking the same trail through the same rock. I stayed up most of that night, too, watched the stars and, in the words of the old spiritual, "looked back in wonder at how I got over" the preceding three years. My mother had died and another relationship had ended. At the church, we'd expanded the sanctuary and mourned the deaths of beloved members. The airplanes had flown into the Twin Towers, and our nation had just gone to war in Iraq. Again, I felt held by those endless stars and that ageless rock.

Another three years and I was again in the heart of the Canyon, this time by a different route. Ten days into the river trip when we descended into that 1.6-billion-year-old Vishnu schist, I felt like I'd come home.

Like other times in the Inner Gorge, I couldn't sleep that night. Same place, same rock, same stars. Different year, different person, different world.

"Return to the deep sources," wrote poet May Sarton. "Nothing less / Will nourish the torn spirit, the bewildered heart, / the angry mind ... nothing less / Will teach the stiff hands a new way to serve, / to carve into our lives the forms of tenderness."[2]

For me, the Grand Canyon as a whole, and the Inner Gorge in particular, are such deep sources. I return to them time and again to nourish my torn spirit and often-bewildered heart and to learn again how to serve and act for love.

I also believe that the liturgical seasons of the church year—Advent, Christmas, Epiphany, Lent, Easter, and Pentecost—can lead us back to such deep sources. Whether we live in New Mexico, New York, or Nebraska, the seasons call us to particular places—Isaiah's exile in Babylon and a stable in Bethlehem, the Jordan River and a wedding in Cana, the courts of Herod and a hill called Calvary. Like hiking the Canyon, the journey to such places is often hard. But also like the Canyon, the deep sources of the Christian seasons hold the promise of healing and strength, even new life.

As we've explored, each individual worship service has a particular structure that leads the congregation into the encounter with God and then out into the world. For Christians, those individual services are also part of a larger whole that leads us through the seasons of the year and also through the life, death, and resurrection of Jesus Christ and the birth of the Christian church.

In the Middle Ages, Christians went on pilgrimages to the holy places of the Christian story—Jerusalem and the Holy Sepulchre, Rome and the site of Peter's death, Santiago de Compostela where the apostle James was buried. For those who couldn't undertake such treks, medieval cathedrals inlaid labyrinths in their transepts as a way to go on pilgrimage to the sacred center without leaving home.

The liturgical year of the Christian church is a "pilgrimage in time." Like those medieval journeys to Jerusalem or the labyrinth's path to the center, the Christian year leads us time and again to the same places. The liturgical seasons invite us to enter into the story and take the journey ourselves, to find our place alongside Moses and Peter, Miriam and Mary, and like them, to find our way home to God, be it from Egypt or the empty tomb.

And like their journeys or my pilgrimage to the heart of the Canyon, the deep places to which we're led on this liturgical journey don't change year after year. But we do, we who gather in Babylon and Bethlehem, Cana and Calvary.

Advent

Come.

The word echoes through the season. "Come, O long-expected Jesus." "Savior of the nations, come."

It expresses our deepest longing. It begins our journey.

"Come, O come, Emmanuel."

"Come, O Wisdom from on high."

"Come, O Dayspring, come and cheer."

"Come, Desire of nations, bind all people in one heart and mind."

Come. The season, and the year, start in waiting and want. But they move to promise:

"Rejoice, rejoice, Emmanuel will come to thee, O Israel."[3]

Finally the word becomes our call to others:

"Come to Bethlehem and see."

"O come, all ye faithful."

Come. It's the word that defines this opening season. Small wonder we call it "Advent," from the Latin *ad-venire*—to come. Four weeks of waiting and preparation for the long-awaited One to come. Four weeks to discern, ponder—most of all be honest about what we really want, and need, come Christmas.

Even more than Lent, its counterpart in color and theme, I think Advent is the hardest season to keep because in Christian worship, the journey to Christmas takes a road much less traveled than that of the outside culture. There is no other time when the church is so out of sync with the rest of the world.

Unlike the retail world's Christmas preparations that start before Halloween, Advent begins a mere four weeks before Christmas. While every shopping mall is adorned in gold and silver, the Christian church clothes itself either in purple (the color of penitence and royalty) or deep sarum blue (the color of the night sky just before dawn, when the morning star appears).

"Silent Night" gets piped into every store and elevator, but in the church we sing a centuries-old plainsong, "O Come, O Come, Emmanuel," and other minor-keyed music. We even try to hold off singing Christmas carols until at least the third Sunday of Advent.

As the world moves into greater darkness toward the winter solstice, museums and zoos offer "light shows." But in Advent worship, we light one candle a week in the Advent wreath, reminding ourselves that we and our world are a "people sitting in darkness," longing for the light to shine.

Even the Advent wreath itself contrasts with the world. The culture revs up for the Christmas rush, but the wreath symbolizes slowing down. It originated when farmers settled in for the winter, took the wheels off their wagons, and laid one down to hold the candles lit against the winter night.

As Christmas becomes more commercialized, the church's Advent journey becomes more important. Not just as a stance against consumerism, but as the only path that truly leads us to the deep sources that will, in the words of May Sarton's poem, "nourish the torn spirit, and bewildered heart."[4]

In the weeks before Christmas, our congregations are filled more than usual with people looking to fill, as Augustine called it, "the God-shaped hole" in their lives. From a pastoral standpoint, those weeks can be difficult for persons who have experienced loss—through death, divorce, downsizing—and who feel very much they are sitting in exile. In addition, the time leading to Christmas can remind us, individually, as a church, even as a nation, how far we have strayed from following the ways of the Prince of Peace.

Keeping Advent helps keep us honest. With its plaintive songs and psalms, deep colors, Scripture lessons longing for hope, even its simple lighting of another candle each week—Advent gives voice and form to our deepest yearnings. In the words of an old hymn, it truly "tells us of the night (and also) what its signs of promise are."[5]

In Advent, make full use of those signs of promise. Despite its competition with the culture, or perhaps because of it, worship in Advent offers a wealth of teachable moments about the meaning of the season and what we're waiting for. The Advent wreath is a good example. The four colored candles each symbolize some part of our longing—for peace, hope, joy, and love. The central candle sums it up as a symbol of Christ, the light that shines in the darkness that the darkness has never overcome.

Even the lighting of the candles can teach. In the first church I served, one with a large sanctuary and long aisles, the Advent candles were lit in silence. Each Sunday, before the call to worship, while the congregation was still settling in and greeting one another, a child would process slowly down the aisle, bearing the light at the end of a long taper. He or she would step cautiously around the heating vents, holding a hand over the flame, determined to keep that little light from going out. Each Sunday, by some miracle, with no announcement that the service was starting, people actually stopped their chatter as they saw the light being carried forward. By the time the child reached the wreath and lit the candle, the sanctuary was in total silence. We had become a people waiting for the light.

The sanctuary where I now serve is much smaller and the congregation generally noisier than those Connecticut Yankees. Since United is often the first entry back into the Christian church for many members, they don't know what Advent is, much less what the candles symbolize. So I designed a litany similar to what our Jewish brothers and sisters use for Passover, when a child asks the meaning of the night and why their people do what they do. The litanies include imagery from the Scripture lessons for the Sunday and seek to link the waiting of the people of Israel in Isaiah's time with our waiting and longing for the same peace and hope in ours. Here is an example from the First Sunday of Advent:

The Lighting of the Advent Candle of Peace:

Why is today different from all other days?

Today is the First Sunday of Advent, and the day we light the first candle on the Advent wreath.

Why do we light candles in this season?

The light from the candles symbolizes the coming of God's light into our world. Each week before Christmas, as the world moves into greater night, we light another candle to proclaim God's light.

What does the first candle mean?

The first candle is the Candle of Peace. It reminds us that the gift of Christmas is the gift of peace, peace in our hearts, peace in our families, even peace in our world.

As we light the first Advent Candle and prepare for the coming of Christ, may we also prepare for peace in every city and every land.

(The first candle is lit.)

Stir up your power and come, O God.[6]
Bring your peace into our world, your word of peace into our waiting.
Stir up your power and come, O God.
Come with your vision of plowshares and pruning hooks.
Come with your call to study war no more.
Come, so that nation shall not lift up sword against nation.
Stir up your power and come, O God.
Come with your passion for peace.
Come with your love for all peoples.
Come with your courage, that we might be open to your coming.
Amen.

For all its solemnity, Advent is also a time of joy and playfulness. As poet Madeline L'Engle affirms:

This is the irrational season,
When love blooms bright and wild.
Had Mary been filled with reason,
There'd have been no room for the child."[7]

At United, we begin Advent services not with the "Alleluia" we use in "Ordinary Time," but often with the jazzy "Prepare Ye the Way" from *Godspell*, sung first by one voice, then the choir, then the whole congregation. The musical's contemporary setting of Isaiah's call lets the congregation know we're starting something new.

Advent also provides an opportunity for the congregation to experience the biblical story firsthand. Even though most Christmas pageants are performed by children dressed up in their parents' bathrobes, Christmas isn't a children's story. In fact, there's only one child in the whole story—and he doesn't have any lines. Instead, it's a story about adults having to make adult decisions. Advent worship can help our adults experience that.

Sometimes in place of the sermon, I've used Advent to introduce the principal characters of the story with short dialogues between them (a.k.a., congregation members dressed in their own bathrobes) and the minister (a.k.a., yours truly). One series was based on the "Songs of the Season," using Isaiah's cry in the wilderness, the canticles of Zechariah and Mary, and the song of the angels to the shepherds. Another Advent series featured people whose words and thoughts we don't know—like Joseph or the Innkeeper—but whose actions are central to the story.

I don't recommend doing such dialogues every year, but having the Christmas characters appear occasionally in the flesh opens up the story in new ways. It also makes the people we often regard as saints (e.g., Mary and Joseph) or sinners (e.g., the innkeeper) far more accessible as the ordinary people they truly were, just like the people of our congregations.

Advent affords opportunities outside of Sunday services to enter into the story. In Northern New Mexico, "Las Posadas" re-creates the journey of Mary and Joseph seeking shelter. Along with a Roman Catholic congregation and an Episcopal church, United hosts one of the nine nights of the journey. We gather at the church and divide into two groups. "Los peregrinos" (the pilgrims), who include two people dressed as Mary and Joseph, stand outside the front door of the church. "Los posaderos" (innkeepers) are on the inside. There's always a lot of good-natured joking about typecasting among the faithful pilgrims and mean innkeepers. "Los peregrinos" start the Las Posadas song, singing for the innkeepers to let them in. "Los posaderos" sing back in Spanish (and read in English): "Go away, you must be robbers and thieves to be out on such a cold night." Even though it's "make-believe," there is something unnerving about telling Mary and Joseph to leave.

The pilgrims finally convince the innkeepers they are who they say they are, the innkeepers open the doors, and everyone processes into the sanctuary for a brief "novena" (prayer service) and more singing. By the time the evening ends, we are ready for Christmas.

Whether with candles and color, Las Posadas or plainsongs, lead your congregation through Advent. Let them experience its depth and its joy. Let them be transformed. Help them change from a people dwelling in deep darkness to a people with the courage to find their way to Bethlehem.

Christmas

Carols. The story from Luke. Candles in the darkness. There's not a whole lot you can do to "improve" a Christmas Eve service. Just stay calm, and let the night and its story do their work.

And if at all possible, in addition to whatever other services you do, try to offer a service specifically designed for families with young children. The warmth of a darkened sanctuary on a cold winter night, the sound of a whole congregation singing songs a child may have only heard at the shopping mall, most of all the mystery and power of that dark sanctuary filled with the light of a hundred candles—those are things a child never forgets.

In those years when because of family problems or finances or both, Christmas seems unlikely to come for some children, such Christmas Eve services can save a child's soul. I know they did mine.

At United, we call it "A Service of Candles and Carols." We sing only two or three verses of the carols and use a simple liturgy that begins:

> Listen, what do you hear?
> (Whispering) *Good news, good news! ¡Noticias buenas! ¡Paz y amor!*
> Angels singing,
> (Softly) *Good news, good news!¡Noticias buenas! ¡Paz y amor!*
> Shepherds coming,
> (Louder) *Good news, good news! ¡Noticias buenas! ¡Paz y amor!*
> Christ is born, Christ is born!
> (Very Loudly) *Good news, good news! ¡Noticias buenas! ¡Paz y amor!*

In place of a sermon, we'll use the Northern New Mexico tale of "The Wise Little Burro" or engage the congregation in a "living" Nativity. It's a light-hearted and fun service, but it introduces children, some of whom have never been in church, to the Nativity story and the mystery of Christmas Eve candle lighting.

On Christmas Eve, we try to connect the child of Bethlehem with the children of our world. The "candles and carols" service includes a litany based on a prayer by Ina Hughes. The repetition makes it easy for children to participate. The leader's part reminds their parents and the rest of us why Christmas is so important.

God of all peoples and places, God of all children of all ages, we come before you this night to offer our prayers for your people. You who were born a child in a world that had no room for you, hear our prayers for the children of this world.

Child of Bethlehem, bless the children.

We pray for children who put chocolate fingers everywhere, who like to be tickled, who stomp in puddles and ruin their pants.

Child of Bethlehem, bless the children.

We pray for children who stare from behind broken screen windows and chain-link fences and who can't bound down the street in a new pair of sneakers.

Child of Bethlehem, bless the children.

We pray for children who bring us sticky kisses and fistfuls of dandelions, who hug us in a hurry and forget their lunch money.

Child of Bethlehem, bless the children.

We pray for children who never get dessert and have no safe blankets to drag behind them.

Child of Bethlehem, bless the children.

We pray for children who spend all their allowance before Tuesday, who shove dirty clothes under the bed, and who can never find their shoes.

Child of Bethlehem, bless the children.

We pray for children whose monsters are real, who aren't spoiled by anybody, and who go to bed hungry.

Child of Bethlehem, bless the children.

We pray for children who squeeze toothpaste all over the sink, who slurp their soup, and whose smiles can make us cry.

Child of Bethlehem, bless the children.

We pray and accept responsibility for children who want to be carried and for those who must, for those we never give up on and for those who don't get a second chance, for those we smother and for those who will grab the hand of anyone kind enough to offer it.

Child of Bethlehem, bless the children.

Child of Bethlehem, we pray for all your children—of this church family and all families. Your love came to us as a child. Give us that love to bless, keep, and hold all your children.

Child of Bethlehem, bless the children. [8]

One last word about Advent and Christmas. Leading a congregation faithfully through these seasons is a tremendous amount of work, especially coupled with the competing covenants with family, friends, and coworkers. Even with that extra preparation, worship may not turn out as we planned or hoped for. The family that was supposed to light the first Advent candle gets sick. The First Sunday of Advent, the congregation wants to sing "Joy to the World" and the Scripture is John the Baptist's call to repent. Half the choir gets laryngitis. *You* get laryngitis.

In such times, I take heart in this season's constant message to Mary, Joseph, the shepherds—and us: "Fear not, the Lord is with you." I also take heart in the story of that first Christmas when Mary got pregnant before the wedding invitations went out, Joseph almost did the wrong thing for the righteous reason, and the Wise Men got lost on the way to Bethlehem. No one was ready. But the Light came anyway that first Christmas.

It will for us as well. Come, O come, Emmanuel.

Epiphany

It comes from a Greek word for "light," and begins with the story of the Wise Men finally "seeing the Light" in the stable in Bethlehem. In many cultures, Epiphany (also "Los Tres Magos" or "Three Kings Day") is even more important than Christmas. At United, we celebrate it not only because of Santa Fe's Hispanic heritage, but also because it's one of the few Christian holy days that hasn't been discovered by Hallmark. Epiphany lets the church get the last word about Christmas.

As a new year begins, Epiphany also reminds us that, like the Magi, no matter how lost we get on the journey to Bethlehem or how dazzled we are by the power and glitter of Jerusalem, we can still go home by another way. That's a powerful word of hope for another year.

The message continues throughout the season. In the depths of winter gloom, the stories of Epiphany tell how the Light spread from Bethlehem into all the world. The Gospel moves from Jesus' baptism at the Jordan to the wedding at Cana to the calling of the disciples in Galilee. Throughout that journey, we proclaim how that Light transformed each place and person, water into wine at Cana, fishermen into disciples at Galilee.

Epiphany comes from the same root as "fantastic," a good word for this season when, as Tony Robinson affirms, "Jesus' teaching, preaching, and healing lit up the world."[9]

Epiphany also challenges us not only to bear witness to that light, but to bear that light to a world that desperately needs it. Like every other season in the Christian year, the movement of Epiphany is from God's story and praise ("I am the Light of the World") to our willingness to respond ("This little light of mine, I'm gonna' let it shine!")

And let it shine! Let the light that filled your sanctuary on Christmas Eve still fill it. Invite your members to bring a candle to put on the altar throughout this season of Light. In preaching and liturgy, identify the Light-bearers of our time, beginning with Martin Luther King Jr., whose birthday comes in this season.

Challenge your congregation to think about the light this world needs. Celebrate how God empowers *them* to be that light—in their work, families, schools, and everyday lives.

On the Sunday you share the story of Jesus' baptism, invite the congregation to renew *their* vows of baptism, their commitment to heed Jesus' call to be the Light of the World. When the story is Jesus' turning water into wine at Cana, encourage them to remember how God has transformed their lives into something deeper than they could ever have imagined. When the Gospel tells how Simon, James, and John left their nets because the light came on for them, have the congregation identify when that has happened for them—those "aha" moments of faith—and how they've responded.

Then lighten your own load of preaching one Sunday, and ask three or four members to share how God has chosen to break into their lives with light and life.

God knows this world can be a pretty dismal place these days. Use Epiphany not just to proclaim the Light, but also to strengthen our trust in it.

Lent will come soon enough. However long it lasts, let Epiphany be a festival of deep light before we enter once again into the shadows of temptation, betrayal, and death.

At the end of the season, you have two choices. The Gospel lesson for the last Sunday of Epiphany is the Transfiguration, when Jesus took three disciples up the mountain and they got a glimpse of the light and glory God has in mind for us and for this world. Dazzling, transfigured, glorious. All words that describe that day. How can you embody them in your worship the last Sunday of the Season of Light?

A second choice for this Sunday, just before Ash Wednesday, is to pull out all the stops and celebrate Mardi Gras, even if you don't live anywhere near New Orleans, and even if Fat Tuesday on a Sunday morning sounds way too hedonistic. Balloons, beads, masks, and music—they all offer innumerable sermon possibilities. More importantly, from Isaiah's messianic "feast of rich food, of well-aged wine" (Is. 25:6) to Jesus' eating with sinners and tax collectors, feasting is at the very heart of our faith. A Jewish friend noted that every Jewish holiday has the same message: "They tried to kill us. They didn't succeed. Let's eat."

The same can be said of the Christian Gospel. The Light of the World knew how to have a good time. It got him into trouble more than once, but it never stopped him. The season that starts right after Mardi Gras leads straight to the Last Supper. It also leads to those resurrection appearances when he was known in the breaking of the bread and in breakfast on the beach. A celebration of Mardi Gras can take us to those places and give us a taste of the feast to come.

The celebration can also be a pilgrimage of music and story to the place that represents Mardi Gras in this country. In these years after Katrina, celebrating Mardi Gras in our churches is a deep and soulful reminder of the question posed by the old Dixieland song: "Do you know what it means to miss New Orleans?"

Whether you lead your congregation up the mountain of Transfiguration or to the streets of New Orleans, let Epiphany end with one last blaze of light, color, and feasting before the solemnity of Lent. You will need that deep source of light to take the journey that lies ahead.

Lent

On the First Sunday of Lent, at Santa Fe's Cathedral Basilica, after the priest has welcomed the congregation, there is a moment of silence, finally broken by the slow beating of a drum. The sound echoes throughout the cathedral, as two men process slowly down the center aisle, carrying a man-sized wooden cross. The pounding of the drum continues until they reach the front of the church, plant the cross in the center of the chancel, and the First Sunday of Lent begins.

The procession is, of course, reminiscent of Jesus' carrying his cross. It also draws on the Penitente traditions of Northern New Mexico. But the procession doesn't simply portray an historical event. This slow, painful walk and the powerful beat of the drum let the worshippers know their own difficult journey has begun.

We may not be quite so dramatic in our UCC settings, but "keeping Lent" is important if Easter is to have meaning. When people enter United's sanctuary on Ash Wednesday or the First Sunday of Lent, they know they've stepped into a different world than just the week before. Gone are the colors and candles of Epiphany and Mardi Gras. No flowers on the altar, just two barren trees on either side. Behind the altar, the banner is purple, the same penitential color of Advent, with a thin red cross in its center. Just as we're invited to give up something for Lent, the sanctuary is stripped-down to its essence throughout the season.

The same is true musically. For six weeks, we neither sing nor say "Alleuia," "Hallelujah," or any other variation of the word. The songs are often in a minor key. The pianist plays a lot of Bach and spirituals. The choirs sing chants or other a capella works.

Some years, the youth present the Gospel lessons in mime, their masked faces and silent actions drawing us deeper into the story than words can alone. Other years, we chant the psalms of Lent and let their lament tell of Jesus' sacrificial journey to Jerusalem.

In the liturgy, we say ancient prayers of confession we seldom use, with phrases like "lost and strayed," "erred from thy ways," "have mercy upon us." They sound harsh and unfamiliar and can make us feel uncomfortable, just like the barrenness of the sanctuary and the dissonance of the music.

And that's the point. When we come to worship in Lent, we know we are in the wilderness and we're going to be there for a while.

Keeping Lent and introducing its symbols or practices into UCC congregations may not be easy. Historically, at least in the Congregational branch of the United Church of Christ, Lent was not observed. In fact, the idea of fasting or using liturgical colors to symbolize the season was often seen as too "Popish" for our Protestant understandings.

Moreover, in many UCC congregations now, we have people from backgrounds where Lent has a variety of negative meanings. A new member of United once said, "In my church, we didn't observe Lent because we'd already given up smoking, dancing, and drinking. *Every* day was Lent!" Another person told me she left her family's tradition and joined United precisely to get away from practices like Lent.

Yet as a pastor, I know how deep is the hunger for healing and wholeness, in the lives of individuals and in this world. I have also learned how the powerful rituals of Lent can offer that healing and wholeness.

My first year out of seminary I was the interim associate chaplain for Yale University. My boss, the senior university chaplain, was a Lutheran who believed strongly in the importance of the liturgical seasons, especially Lent.

He also believed that Ash Wednesday should include a service of "confession and absolution" and that his associate (I) needed to help lead it. After the sermon, the congregation would be invited to come forward to one of us to offer their confession and receive absolution and the imposition of ashes.

It was a stretch, but I could deal with the ashes. Granting absolution was another matter, and I almost lost my job over it. I argued long and hard with my boss, trying to explain that personal confession and absolution were not part of my UCC understanding, either of the relationship with God or the role of the clergy. It was an argument I had to lose to keep my job. So that evening, during the time of confession and absolution, I stood with my little container of ashes and prayed no one would come forward to my station.

But they did. I knew almost every one of them. Students whom I'd counseled. Faculty I'd had coffee with. Administrative support staff with whom I'd collated, stapled, and stuffed envelopes. People who had told me their stories, often difficult ones of broken relationships, fears that kept them from completing their dissertations, family problems. I had listened to them in my office, the dining hall, or the local coffee house. I believe I listened well. But now something moved them to come to this Ash Wednesday service and to come forward for confession and absolution.

Some congregants confessed what was on their hearts, others simply said, "You know why I'm here." With each of them, I put one hand on their shoulder, dipped my other into the ashes, and marked their foreheads as I said, "Beloved, from dust you have come to dust you shall return. Receive these ashes and know that God hears your confession. In the name of Jesus Christ, you are forgiven. Go in peace."

By the end of the service, I was exhausted. I also had to acknowledge the senior chaplain's wisdom. The ritual of confession and absolution did what even my deepest, most compassionate pastoral listening couldn't do. It offered, through the ritual and my role as priest *and* pastor, an acceptance by God and a reconnection to God. It was a powerful way to begin the Lenten journey to new life.

At United, we haven't gone so far as to initiate a ritual of confession and absolution, but we do observe Ash Wednesday, complete with ashes. When we began the service several years ago, I knew it had to speak to people who either had degrading memories of Lent or who knew nothing about the season, other than cultural stereotypes.

Lent is traditionally a time of giving up things—meat, chocolate, alcohol—as a way of participating in Jesus' sacrifice. It is also when we seek to deepen our relationship with God. United's first Ash Wednesday service combined those two intentions. I found a small clay fireplace to put in the center of the sanctuary. Inserted in each bulletin was a blank piece of paper. In the sermon, I emphasized that in Lent we give up those things that keep us from the fullness of the relationship with God. That could be something tangible, like chocolate or alcohol. It could also be intangible old fears, long-held anger, or ancient grudges.

After the sermon and before the imposition of ashes, people were invited to write down what they want to give up. Then they came forward to put their paper in the fireplace, letting those fears, grudges, and hurts turn back to dust and ashes. If they chose, they could then step to the side and be marked with ashes, praying that God would strengthen them in their Lenten resolve.

One final word about the power of Ash Wednesday. It not only prepares us for the journey of Lent, but it also reminds us of the whole journey of our lives, particularly of our mortality and that of the people we love and serve in our congregations. "From dust, we have all come. To dust we shall all return."

That reminder is neither pleasant nor desirable. "Dust to dust, ashes to ashes" runs counter to our culture's focus on youth and good looks. But with that reminder of death comes also the reminder of the One who holds our lives.

On Ash Wednesday 2002, Bob came forward to receive the ashes as he had for the previous ten years at United and throughout his childhood and youth as a Roman Catholic. Bob served on our Church Council, chaired the Finance Team, took the kids camping, and painted the walls of the new Nurture Center. Only a few years older than me, Bob was a foot taller. I stood on tiptoe to reach his forehead, but he still had to bend down to receive.

A leading environmentalist, Bob spent a lot of times outdoors. His weather-beaten skin felt rough as I made the sign of the cross on his forehead. "Beloved, from dust you have come. To dust you shall return. Go in peace, my brother."

Two weeks later on another Wednesday night, Bob suffered a massive brain aneurysm. He lay in a coma for three days as his wife made decisions about life support and organ donation, and his family gathered from around the country.

On Friday, before the life support was ended, I joined the family in the ICU room. The respirator continued its rhythmic breathing as we sang hymns, read Scripture, and prayed. I anointed Bob's forehead with oil, just as I had marked it with ashes a few days before. This time I was the one who bent down to the hospital bed.

Five days later on a cold March afternoon, as Bob's coffin was lowered into the ground, I said the same words I had on Ash Wednesday. "Ashes to ashes. Dust to dust. Go in peace. Amen."

There's not been an Ash Wednesday since when I don't think of Bob or remember the lesson of Lent 2002. "Beloved,from dust we have all come. To dust we shall all return. Go in peace, my brother."

Holy Week

Over the years at United, we have gradually built the liturgy of Holy Week. Initially the church had a Palm Sunday celebration, a small Maundy Thursday service in which the community gathered around a table, and two Easter Sunday services.

My first year, the Worship Team and I decided to change the format of the Maundy Thursday service to accommodate a larger gathering than could fit around the single table. With their permission, I also added a Good Friday service. Less than a dozen people came, but despite the small number, I felt it was important to begin a tradition of a fuller Holy Week, one that didn't simply go from the Palm Sunday celebration to Easter, but instead took the journey through the back streets of Jerusalem and beyond the city walls to Calvary.

The journey begins with the Palm Sunday processional, as the children march around the sanctuary waving palms and singing "Hosanna." But after they leave, the service turns a corner and focuses on what happened after the cheering stopped. We may begin with "All Glory, Laud and Honor," but we end Palm Sunday with "Journey to Gethsemane."

As in Advent, we share some of the Holy Week journey with our Catholic and Episcopal brothers and sisters—a Passover Seder led by the Rabbi or Cantor from the Temple, an ecumenical, and almost medieval, Wednesday Tenebrae based solely on the Psalms.

Maundy Thursday

The name comes from the Latin *mundatum*, meaning "commandment," for it's a night we remember the new commandment Jesus gave his disciples: "To love one another." At the end of the service, after a brief homily and the sharing of Communion, we use the Tenebrae (Latin for "shadows") to remind us of the full extent of that love.

Communion ends, and all the lights go off, except for seven candles on the Communion table. Behind them stand seven readers, generally youth or young adults. One by one, they read a part of the Passion story, extinguish a candle, and sit down. The sixth reading ends with Jesus' being led away for crucifixion. By the light of the remaining candle, the last person reads the prologue from the Gospel of John: "The light shines in the darkness and the darkness did not overcome it." Then he or she extinguishes the last flame.

The congregation sits in darkness and silence until I or another leader starts the Lord's Prayer and they join in. More silence. A lone voice sings "Were You There When They Crucified My Lord?" More silence.

The Maundy Thursday service has no benediction. After "Were You There?" the congregation leaves when they choose, scattering into the gloom, even as the disciples all went their own way into their night.

Good Friday

Like Maundy Thursday, worship on Good Friday is not just the retelling or enactment of that day two thousand years ago. It is also the story of Good Friday here and now, so there are a number of ways to engage that story. Sometimes we've simply read the whole Passion from one of the Gospels, with silent interludes to let the congregation think about what they've heard. For several years in Santa Fe, I organized an ecumenical Good Friday service that incorporated the traditional "seven last words of Christ" with the writings of people who, like Jesus, had given their lives for others—e.g., Martin Luther King Jr., Archbishop Oscar Romero, Mother Theresa. Another year, we read current news stories alongside the story of Jesus' forgiveness, despair, and faith.

Good Friday is also an opportunity to take the journey literally. New Haven's Downtown Cooperative Ministry offered a community "Stations of the Cross" service that processed around the city to places of need and of service—the city jail, the corporate headquarters for Electric Boat, city hall, the local soup kitchen. The procession connected Jesus' journey to the cross, with its scenes of injustice, hope, and human frailty, with such places in the immediate community of New Haven.

In the mid-1990s, thanks to the invitation of a Roman Catholic colleague, I shared leadership with the archbishop in a service that integrated the Stations of the Cross with "A Witness for Persons with AIDS." Held at the newest of the Roman Catholic parishes, the service used the traditional litany of the stations—"Jesus condemned, Jesus carries the cross, Jesus falls for the first time"—followed by a brief reflection from a person with AIDS, or their loved ones, and a prayer. The actual journey was only around the inside of a church, but the sacred journey took us back to Jesus' ordeal and also to the present suffering of our brothers and sisters.

At United, we offer yet another way of taking the Good Friday journey. Members and friends, especially youth and children, gather early that morning for a circle of prayer and then go to a Habitat site or other place of service. As Jesus offered himself totally for the sake of this world that first Good Friday, we seek to offer ourselves to the wider community. The group works through the morning and then returns to the church to join in the noontime service.

In 2006, the Good Friday journey took a different form. People still went to work at Habitat, but beginning at 6:00 that morning, we also held a six-hour "Good Friday Vigil of Remembrance." In many Christian churches, vigil is kept from Good Friday morning through the dawn of Easter, as members sit silently in the sanctuary to "keep watch" from the darkness of Good Friday to Easter Dawn. United's Vigil had an express purpose. From before dawn on Good Friday and continuing until the noontime service, people from the congregation read the names, ages, and hometowns of the almost three thousand U.S. service men and women who had died in the Afghanistan and Iraq Wars since October 2001. At the end of each half hour segment, the reader offered a prayer for the dead and their families and also for the countless unnamed Afghanis and Iraqis who had died. People were invited to come at any time during the vigil and to stay as long as they chose.

In explaining the service, the Youth Minister Gary Reyes noted that traditionally on Good Friday, we remember the life and death of Jesus Christ, the Prince of Peace who gave his life for others. We also acknowledged that our country is in the midst of a war, but there have been few public services or rituals that would allow us to mourn the dead, on all sides, and also to pray for peace. It felt appropriate to do so on the day Christians confess the consequences of hate and fear and also proclaim the One whose love overcame, and still overcomes, that hate and fear.

The readers ranged in age from fourteen to seventy-four. Some were veterans of other wars, two had been conscientious objectors. One woman's husband had gone ashore on D-Day. Another's had served in Vietnam. Some readers were Democrats, some Republican. Some had supported the initial invasion of Iraq. Others had opposed it.

The service began in darkness. By the end of the first hour of four hundred names, I and others were in tears. Each name sounded like one more nail being pounded into the cross. With each name and hometown, I felt we were there with the grieving family and a community in mourning, just as we are asked to be there at the foot of the Golgotha cross.

I had committed myself to staying through the full six hours to bear witness and support the readers, but I wasn't sure I could make it through all that grief. Then the dawn slowly began to lighten the room. With it came an amazing sound. One by one, the birds outside began their morning song. As the reader continued with the grievous litany of death, more birds began to sing. It was as though God was speaking through creation, breaking into the vigil to remind us who gets the last word, even on Good Friday. To remind us, too, that Word is Life, even on Good Friday.

Yet even with the birds' singing, I was never so glad to see a service end as when I, the last reader, finished the list of names as of April 9, 2006. Even after the vigil was over, readers and congregants alike continued to feel disoriented and upset. Authentic worship can do that to us at times.

I also know I couldn't wait to get to Easter and the "Hallelujah Chorus." After all that death, we needed Easter's infusion of life and God's triumph over the worst we humans can do, then and now.

One last word about this week. Offering the services of Holy Week is demanding and involves intense preparation. Over eight days, we have nine different services, each with its own bulletin, sanctuary set-up, liturgists, and music. Holy Week requires other preparations as well—the practical tasks of ordering palms and Easter lilies and also the hard ones of assembling the names of the war dead for the Good Friday vigil or composing the Easter lilly memorial list.

It would be more practical to go directly from Palm Sunday to Easter. It would also be easier emotionally to forego the remembrance of the days, and nights, between the two celebrations. Betrayal, denial, being forsaken by one's friends and accused falsely by one's enemies. Weeping for the death of a friend, facing the awful emptiness that comes after a death. Most all, wondering where in God's name God *is*. Those are the days and services of Holy Week.

Why not just skip them and get to Easter?

I encourage you not to do so. Despite the extra preparation and the difficulty of the journey, I'm glad we mark the days of Holy Week. Not because I'm a martyr, but because I'm glad that *all* the days of that week, not just

Palm Sunday and Easter Sunday, are holy. God was there every day.

Each year, some people in the congregation are eager for Easter morning. Life is going well, full of new life and possibilities, and Easter is chance to celebrate all that goodness.

But I also know each year there are others who know more the fear and bewilderment of Maundy Thursday's impending grief than Easter's joy. The people we serve, or we ourselves, may feel more at home on Good Friday than on Easter because in our lives, the lives of loved ones, or the life of this world, it feels like Good Friday every day of the week.

The good news of Holy Week is that God was *present* every day of that week—from Palm Sunday to Easter morning and all the difficult, fearful, empty days in between. The equally good news of Holy Week is that God knew intimately the sorrow and sense of abandonment we can also know in our days that seem anything but holy. The services of Holy Week remind us of that truth and also that God is *still* present, every day of every week, in your life, in my life, and even in the life of this world.

Take time to take the journey from Palm Sunday through Maundy Thursday to Good Friday, and know that God is with you and your congregation every step of the way. Holy Week can change your experience of Easter. It may even change your life.

Easter!

I admit, I am a fervent believer in Easter sunrise services, even if means getting up at 4:00 a.m. to do three services. As a teenager, there were times when the only thing I could believe about Easter and resurrection was that the sun would rise that day. As a pastor, I believe the sunrise service is an important outreach to the wider community. For people who may not feel they "fit in" with a church nor feel particularly resurrected, a sunrise service offers a way to experience the message of Easter even with great doubt.

The service doesn't need to be long, you don't need an in-depth sermon. Just get people together outdoors, sing "Morning Has Broken" and "Christ the Lord Is Risen Today" (even a capella), read the Gospel, and let God and this good earth show you the possibility of new life at dawn.

At United, we begin in our outdoor "celebration circle" that can symbolize the tomb. Someone reads the story of the women going to anoint the body. Then we sing a simple "Alleluia" as we walk up to where we can see the sun rise. We share Communion, have short prayers and sing fast, because generally it's pretty cold.

Like Christmas, a challenge of Easter is, of course, the number of people who come only for that part of the journey. Therefore, in all the Easter services, I do three things. One, I acknowledge that many of us come to Easter with great doubt, be it about God, the holy day we're celebrating, or our own faith journeys. I think it's important to give people permission to doubt, even as we celebrate with great joy and affirm new possibilities. (However, don't do what one new minister did who preached his first Easter sermon on "Why I Don't Believe in the Resurrection." Not surprisingly, it was also his *last* Easter sermon.)

Two, in the welcoming of visitors, I express our hope they will be fed by the service—and also leave hungry for more of what they found by sharing worship in a community of faith.

Three, we structure the Easter services to recall the journey that brought us to this day. The indoor services begin with the sanctuary lights off. After the announcements and greeting, there is a time of silence. Then the liturgist reads the Gospel story of Palm Sunday. The choir sings a verse of "All Glory Laud and Honor." Then silence and a reading from the Passion. The pianist plays one verse of "O Sacred Head Now Wounded" or a solo voice sings one verse of "Were You There?" Silence again. Then a different solo voice softly begins the "Caribbean Hallelujah" (in *The New Century Hymnal*) or similar song. The choir joins in the second time around. Then the whole congregation stands and sings the first "Hallelujahs" and "Alleluias" we've sung in six weeks. The lights come on, and Easter really begins.

Even if you're in a small church, make Easter big and get as many "Hallelujahs" and "Alleluias" into the service as possible. After the minor keys and solemn music of Lent, we need the blessings of those Hallelujahs. It's what the heavenly chorus of Revelation sings, what inspired Georg Frederic Handel, bankrupt, ill, and almost blind, to proclaim that as he composed his "Hallelujah Chorus": "I do believe I have seen all of Heaven before me, and the great God Himself."[10]

My first Easter at United, we ended both services with a congregational singing of the "Hallelujah Chorus." It made no sense to do so. We had scraped together some funds for a Sunday pianist, and a volunteer had offered to direct a pickup choir. Still we were averaging only twenty in the early service and less than a hundred in the other. But it was Easter, the worship committee was game, so we decided to try it in both services.

I first heard an entire congregation sing the "Hallelujah Chorus" at Riverside Church my last Easter in seminary. William Sloane Coffin led the singing. At First Church in Middletown, we also used it as the final statement on Easter. Over those years, I experienced Handel's chorus not simply as a great piece of music nor a way to pull out all the stops when the church was packed, but also as a deeply pastoral experience for many people.

At First Church, during the final Easter hymn (usually "Thine Is the Glory," to get another Handel tune in our ears), people came forward from the congregation to join the choir. Once everyone was assembled, and before the benediction, a leader read the necrology, the names of members and friends who had died since the previous Easter. There was a moment of silence. Then the organist launched into the opening chords of the "Hallelujah Chorus."

I had sung *Messiah* many times before I got to First Church, but it never had the depth as when we sang it after hearing those names on Easter morning. My first year, I stood in the midst of the altos singing all those "forevers and evers" and seeing a young couple whose three-month-old baby girl had been named in the necrology. Three years later, I looked out at a good friend who had sung in the choir with her husband and who was the alto I always stood next to. She didn't come forward to sing that Easter. Her husband had been killed by a drunk driver two weeks before Christmas, and she hadn't sung since then. But there she stood, tears streaming down her face, singing with us from her pew, "Hallelujah, Hallelujah, Hallelujah. And He shall reign forever and ever. Hallelujah!"

I knew what the "Hallelujah Chorus" did for the people of First Church. I believed it could do the same for United. I also knew it was crazy to try to do. For one, our new pianist had informed me she didn't like Easter. A rather morose person, her favorite key was minor and Lent her favorite season. But we were paying her salary, minimal as it was, so she had rehearsed with the pickup choir a couple times. I still had hopes we could pull it off.

Second, Easter that year was the first Sunday of daylight savings time, as in "set your clocks ahead an hour." I wasn't too concerned when the pianist hadn't shown up by the start of the morning's choir rehearsal. When she still wasn't there a half hour later and the choir was beginning to murmur, it suddenly dawned on me what had happened. Sure enough, when I called her house, I got her out of bed. Half asleep, she protested she had a full hour before the service started. I mentioned daylight savings, she gasped, and I went out to the congregation to tell them that we were going to start Easter a bit late.

Nonetheless, at the end of the service, we passed out the music and that little group of fifty people sang the "Hallelujah Chorus." We sang it again at the late service. We've sung it every Easter since then.

As happened at First Church, there are some years when the necrology list is too long with too many names of beloved friends and young people. Even those years, perhaps especially in those years, we sing the "Hallelujah Chorus" anyway, forever and ever and ever. Ha-le-lu-jah!

Handel's *Messiah* is one way to end Easter. There are many others. At the end of the three-hour Easter vigil at St. Francis Cathedral, when the priest proclaims, "Easter has begun!" the packed congregation turns to each other and gives high fives!

I don't know what the Pope would say, but after the long journey of Lent, high fives seem pretty sacramental to this Protestant!

Eastertide

The Bulgarians and Belarusians call it "The Great Day." The Greeks and Armenians say it's "Resurrection." The Hungarian and Estonian words for it mean "buying meat." In many cultures, it's some variation of *Pasque* (*Pascua* in Spanish), from the Hebrew *Pescha*, or Passover.

"It" is Easter, a name first used in the eighth century. The English title for the day derives from Eostre, the Teutonic goddess of fertility whose symbol, appropriately, was the rabbit. Hence, the Eostre Bunny.

But it's the Koreans, who call it "Resurrection Season," and the Latvians and Lithuanians who name it "The Great Days" who get it right. By any name, Easter is a *season*, not just one day but fifty days of feasting and celebrating new life, ten days longer than Lent—which tells us something about the true priorities of the Christian church. More feasting than fasting. Hallelujah!

Make the most of the time. Keep singing the "Alleluias" and "Hallelujahs." Keep watering the lilies in the sanctuary. Most of all, keep proclaiming the stories. Use the appointed lessons from Acts to tell how that first Easter empowered the disciples and women to do things they never thought they could. Don't confine the transforming power of Easter to one day. It took Peter, Mary Magdalene, and the others the rest of their lives to understand what happened not just to Jesus but to all of them that day of resurrection.

Helping our congregations believe in, much less trust, the resurrection (both Jesus' and theirs) isn't easy, especially in our time. In *High Tide in Tucson*, essayist Barbara Kingsolver describes how she came back "from the colorless world of despair by forcing myself to look, hard, for a long time at a single glorious thing: a flame of red geranium outside my bedroom window. And then another: my daughter in a yellow dress . . .Until I learned to be in love with my life again.

"Like a stroke victim retraining new parts of the brain to grasp lost skills," she continues, "I have taught myself joy, over and over again."[11]

Use the fifty days of Eastertide to learn how to be in love with life again.

We know the disciplines of Lent: fasting, abstinence, prayer. Training ourselves to trust life, to know joy, requires just as much discipline.

Life goes on after Easter Sunday. Sometimes that can be a terrible thing. It was the Thursday after Easter 1995 that Timothy McVeigh drove a truck filled with nitrous fertilizer to the Murrow Federal Building in Oklahoma City and detonated it, killing 168 people, including children at play in the day care center.

At United that Sunday we used the liturgy and Easter hymns we'd planned earlier in the week. The call to worship, from the *Book of Worship*, affirmed that God is the one "who gathers up the fragments of our lives and creates new possibilities." We had no idea how appropriate that liturgy would be for the Second Sunday of Easter 1995.

Life goes on after Easter. It is our responsibility in worship to proclaim time and again who gets the last word *and* that the Word is *life*. Our congregations, and our world, need Easter to be more than a one-day event. The fifty days of Eastertide keep returning us to the stories and songs of resurrection. Worship in Eastertide focuses on breaking bread or breakfast on the beach—ordinary things, like Kingsolver's red geranium or her daughter's yellow dress—that can help bring us back to life over and again.

"Practice resurrection," affirms poet Wendell Berry.[12] We have fifty days of Easter to do just that.

Pentecost

The temptation, of course, is to stop with Easter. But the journey continues, and any Sunday that includes tongues of fire and the mighty wind of God's Spirit is worth celebrating.

It's also good to be reminded that something as ordinary as our churches had such extraordinary beginnings.

There isn't much set ritual around Pentecost nor many cultural expectations. That means you can have fun with it. Don't just settle for reading the Scripture in different languages. Make it a great celebration. Include the children. Ask people to wear red—the color of the Spirit. Adorn the sanctuary with red balloons and red flowers. When the story of Pentecost is read, stop after each line and invite the congregation to do what story says happened. Make a sound "like the rush of a mighty wind." Put red strips of paper in the bulletin to use as the "tongues of fire." Greet one another in a language other than your own. Turn to one another and proclaim a "mighty deed of God" you've experienced just the past week.

Most of all, have the sons and daughters of the congregation share their visions and the old ones tell their dreams. That's the spirit of Pentecost, a spirit our churches need.

The Season of Pentecost (Ordinary Time) or "The Season of the Church"

As a season, Pentecost presents a variety of challenges, not the least of which is its length. Depending on Easter's date, Pentecost stretches from seven to eight months and covers three climate seasons. That's a lot of "ordinary time." The season also includes three months of summer, when people leave town and in some parts of the country, churches shut down.

A second challenge is a lack of direction to the season. Advent heads straight for Bethlehem, Lent to Jerusalem, but Pentecost? It's not clear where it heads. After the first Pentecost, even the disciples went in different directions.

Third, there is no one dramatic storyline, culminating in birth or resurrection. True, Pentecost celebrates the birth of the Christian church, but that probably didn't make the evening news. Moreover, the season of Pentecost focuses on what happened next, namely the exasperating, hard, messy work of being the church. Paul's arguments with Peter about who's welcome at the table don't have quite the drama of Jesus' trial before Pilate.

Fourth, lots of national and cultural holidays occur during the season: Memorial and Veterans' Days, Mother's and Father's Days. With them comes the expectation that worship should pay them homage.

Yet these challenges can be turned into opportunities if we keep in mind the central purpose of Pentecost: the shaping of a people to be the People of God.

Pentecost is long because it takes a long time to do that. After the first Passover and the Exodus out of Egypt, the people of Israel had to wander in the wilderness for four decades until they were ready for the promised land. After the first Pentecost, it took Peter, Mary, and the others the rest of their lives to create the Christian church.

Is it any wonder that Pentecost—this "Season of the Church"—is the longest of the year?

Just as the other half of the year goes from Advent to Epiphany to Lent to Easter, break Pentecost into smaller units, each with a particular focus with the overall goal of creating a "people fit for God."

The season lends itself to that rhythm. Pentecost generally begins as the school year ends. The early weeks of Pentecost are often filled with graduations, confirmation, and end of the year children's ministry programs. All are great opportunities to commission children and youth to be the sons and daughters of the Pentecost prophesy as they enter into the next stages of their lives.

Similarly in many local churches, Pentecost coincides with annual meetings and the election of new officers. In worship, call the new leaders forward, lay hands on them, and pray God's Spirit be poured upon them so they can find their place among those first apostles, the men and women who received a Spirit powerful enough to create the church and change the world.

Turn the challenge of the summer months, with their erratic attendance, into an opportunity to focus on some of the individual Spirit-filled people of our biblical tradition. It's a great way to let new lay leaders know what they've just said "yes" to.

Some possibilities:

Do a worship series on the minor prophets like Joel, Micah, Obadiah, and Jonah. Who were they and what did they say? Who were the people they were trying to reach? How did they respond? How did they feel about being *minor* prophets? What does that tell us about being leaders and Christians today?

Focus on Peter and his struggles to be faithful in this new Christian way. Or focus on Paul, one of the people Peter struggled with.

Choose some of the other first Christians in Acts, who don't get much press. People like the Ethiopian eunuch who asks Peter to baptize him (even before he goes to his first new member class) or the slave girl of Philippi whom Paul "heals" because she's a pest.

Use the season's natural pull to travel as a theme for Spirit-led journeys, be it the wanderings of Abraham and Sarah, the desert sojourn of Moses and the Hebrews, or the journeys of Paul and Silas. How did their journeys shape their faith?

Explore the places they lived in or wandered to. Ur. Niveneh. Sinai. Ethiopia. They're all places in the news these days, largely because of the war in Iraq and other conflicts in the Middle East. Someone once said, "War is the way Americans learn geography." Use the Bible instead.

Reframe the national and cultural holidays that mark the church's Pentecost time. Another name for the season is "Kingdom Time" or "Realm of God Time." Look at Memorial Day or the Fourth of July through that lens. What does it mean, as a nation and as citizens, to have God's Spirit poured out upon us? What dreams and visions does God call us to have for our country and the world?

Similarly, "baptize" the cultural holidays of Mother's Day and Father's Day. The UCC already renamed Mother's Day as "The Festival of the Christian Home" (which prompted a former choir director to rename Father's Day as "The Festival of the Christian Garage"). Use the secular holidays of the family to affirm what it means to be the *new* family of God, bound by the Spirit of God, rather than biology or bloodline.

When the summer ends and people regather for school, work, soccer, football, and sometimes even church, mark that new beginning in worship. In a church I served, the second Sunday of September began with the sound of the shofar, the way our Jewish brothers and sisters are called together at the beginning of Roshashana, their new year.

In Santa Fe, the second weekend of September is traditionally Las Fiestas, a similar time of family reunions, feasting, dancing, and worship. Whether with mariachi trumpets or Jewish shofars, sound the call and regather your congregation for a new year of being the People of God.

Pentecost worship in the fall is regathering with a purpose, namely to let ourselves be shaped anew by God's Spirit and Word. Use the time to recommit to being not just the individuals but the community God calls us to be. Bless the children at the beginning of a new year in children's ministry. Bless their teachers, too. Present the first, fourth, and seventh graders their Bibles, along with a piece of candy, just as a Jewish child gets a taste of honey when he or she first learns to read the Torah to be reminded of the sweetness of God's Word.

For the whole congregation, consider a "service of the renewal of baptismal and membership vows" to remember the promises we once made to resist evil and seek new life as Christ's disciples.

Throughout the fall, use stories like the exodus or the travels of Jesus to keep gathering the people. Maybe celebrate Pentecost again before you start the fall stewardship campaign, in case the congregation has forgotten what it feels like to be empowered by God's Spirit or your dreams and visions are a bit cloudy.

Use each Sunday in Pentecost to remind your congregation of God's extraordinary Spirit, even in Ordinary Time.

The season of Pentecost can feel like the long, flat water stretches of the river trip when we longed for the excitement of the rapids. But those stretches were an important part of the journey. John Wesley Powell said on his first trip through the Grand Canyon in 1869 that the Canyon was a "library of the gods." "The shelves are not for books," he continued, "but form the stony leaves of one great book. He who would read the language of the universe may dig out letters here and there . . . and read, in a slow and imperfect way, but still so as to understand a little, the story of creation."[13] The still water stretches on the river gave us time, like Powell, to read that book and reflect on the eons of creation we were passing through.

In the church, Pentecost worship offers a similar opportunity to read and reflect on the book we call the Bible, to explore its layers of meaning, and the people and journeys we find there, so as, to paraphrase Powell, to understand a little the story of creation as well as the Creator.

Still water stretches of the river also gave us time to tell stories, play together, even engage in a few water fights. For a novice like me, still water was a chance to practice rowing and build some muscle for the journey.

Likewise, the ordinary Sundays of Pentecost can create us anew as a community. They can help us build the strength and courage we need for our ministries in the church and the world. The season may not have the intense drama of Advent or Lent nor does Ordinary Time lead to Bethlehem or Jerusalem. Still, if we honor it, the long months of Pentecost have the potential to lead us deeper into community with one another, deeper into communion with God, and deeper also into the world around us—just as that first Pentecost led Peter, Mary, and the others into community and out into the world.

If we do our work right, worship in Pentecost can do one more thing. And that is to create in us and in our communities such a hunger for God's presence that we can't wait for the waiting of Advent to begin.

"Return to the deep sources," counsels May Sarton. "Nothing less will nourish the torn spirit, the bewildered heart."[14] Nothing less will teach us "a new way to serve."

Return to the deep seasons of the Christian church, and they too will nourish our spirits and hearts and teach us again how to love, year after year after year.

Six

The Word as Sacrament: Preaching

"She is a friend of my mind. She gather me, man.
The pieces I am, she gather them and give them back to me
in all the right order. It's good, you know, when you got a woman
who is a friend of your mind."

—Sixto about his Thirty-Mile Woman in Toni Morrison's *Beloved*[1]

hese rapids here," said Chris, the trip leader, pointing to the river book, "are Horn Creek. The book says we should be okay since the water is so high, but we should still scout it. My first time on the river, we portaged it because the rocks were too exposed."

Further down, Chris read from the book again. "Coming up are Hermit Rapids. The book says to run river right and watch out for the big eddy on the left." She looked up from the guide. "The book's right," she said. "I got stuck there for an hour."

A good guidebook and a leader to interpret it helped us understand the river and navigate our way through its rapids, channels, and eddies. A good sermon can do the same in the rest of our lives.

A good sermon also does more. Along with telling us where the rapids are or how many miles to the next campsite, it tells us who we are on this journey, what we're looking for, and why we're taking it in the first place.

Like Morrison's "Thirty-Mile Woman," a good sermon gathers us, gathers the pieces of our minds, and gives them back to us in all the right order.

A sermon reminds us how far we've come and where we're headed. Most of all, it dares to speak of the One who is the source of it all—the river, the travelers, and the journey itself. And it reminds us over and again that if we're willing to trust that Source with nothing less than our lives, then neither we or our traveling companions will ever be the same.

As much I am fed by ritual and liturgy (to the point that Monsignor Jerome Martinez, rector of St. Francis Cathedral Basilica, calls me a "closet Catholic"), I am glad to be a Protestant with our historic emphasis on the preached Word. As a kid, I loved learning Bible stories, not because of their moral teachings, but because the characters always got into trouble and God always still loved them. That gave me hope. As a teenager, the sermons of Martin Luther King Jr. and William Sloan Coffin made the ancient biblical texts come alive with passion and meaning. Their sermons offered a new perspective on Jesus Christ, who he was, who he *is*, and what it means to follow in his way.

Through the preaching of people like King, Coffin, and the minister of my local UCC church, I experienced how preaching can transform a life—my own. They showed God at work in the world in a different way from what I had been taught. In my family's theology, along with a wonderful sense of awe at creation, a strong sense of caring for others, and a never-ending curiosity, was sometimes the belief that God caused suffering to teach us lessons and make us stronger. But the sermons I heard as a teenager spoke of a God who stood with us in suffering and whose intent for this world and for each individual was not hurt, but wholeness; not oppression or abuse, but justice and right relationship. That also gave me hope, just like those Bible stories of my childhood.

I know, perhaps as you do, there have been sermons that saved my life. The preached Word that opened Scripture in a new way, spoke a word of grace or forgiveness that I needed to hear, or offered an understanding of resurrection that truly offered new life.

Yes, I am very glad to be Protestant and very glad that a major part of worship is engagement with the lively and transforming Word of God. I trust you are, too.

Probably because I grew up in a teacher's family, I learned early on that words and ideas were, if not sacramental in a formal sense, certainly sacred. My mother used her bulletin to take notes on a sermon, so she could think about it later. I could always tell when she didn't think much of a preacher or his sermon. No notes.

This may seem a rather odd upbringing and an odd way to approach worship, especially if the focus is connecting us with the mystery of God. But from her passion for knowledge and understanding, I found that mystery could be mediated not only through great ritual and weekly sacraments, but also through mere words.

Of course, not just any words, but ones that were well-chosen and thoughtful, words that drew deeply from the biblical texts and also from the best that literature, science, psychology, or political thought had to offer. Most of all, words that were alive and that showed the preacher truly loved God "with all heart, soul, and mind" and wanted us to do the same.

Much of the recent conversation about preaching, like much of the discussion about worship in general, has often been polarized into assessing sermons as either "thinking" or "feeling," coming from the head or from the heart. But to neglect either weakens our preaching. A sermon full of passion but without thoughtfulness can be as boring as an intellectual one with no passion. I knew with either kind, I'd see my mother put down her pen.

As pastors and leaders of local congregations, our preaching has a lot of competition these days. We're up against megachurch televangelists with megastaffs to take care of the buildings, budgets, small groups, counseling, and everything else that eats into sermon preparation time like a caterpillar on a tomato plant. Moreover, from Judge Judy to Dr. Phil, lots of people are dispensing advice. Both the TV therapists and the TV preachers have access to thousands more people than you or I probably ever will. Plus they've got make-up artists to make them look good and techies to make them sound good.

It's enough to make a local church preacher turn in her ordination papers. What keeps me from doing so (and I pray will keep you as well) are the three things I find every time I open Scripture. One, the lively Word of God that never ceases to surprise, challenge, and comfort—sometimes all at the same time. Two, the countless examples from Moses and Amos to Mary Magdalene and Paul of people who proclaimed the Word of God, were themselves transformed by that Word, wrestled with it, preached it to seemingly deaf ears, and ultimately changed the world with their proclamation. Three, the model of that Word embodied in the life and preaching of Jesus Christ.

It is his model that I offer here for preaching. I do so because, in the words of the spiritual, when "I get discouraged and think my work's in vain," I do what the song says to do—go back to the Word itself, not only to be revived by the Spirit or to "tell the love of Jesus" but also to learn again from him what to preach, how to prepare for it, and why it's important.

What to Preach? Nothing Less than the Kingdom of God

A rather audacious claim, to be sure, and one that has taken me a good many years to be able to say out loud. But it's right there in Scripture, and the need for it has never been greater in our world.

According to the earliest Gospel, Mark, the first thing Jesus did when he came out of the wilderness was to preach, "proclaiming the good news of God, and saying 'The time is fulfilled, the kingdom of God has come near; repent, and believe the good news'" (1:14–15).

He proclaimed that even before he healed a single person, turned water into wine, ate with sinners and tax collectors, or offered any other tangible signs of that kingdom. Yes, that kingdom was at hand in his power to heal, in his reaching out to the outcasts, in his respect for women, Samaritans, and other unclean people, in his care for the poor. But from the beginning, that kingdom was also at hand in his preaching. He didn't just proclaim the kingdom. He created it with his words. And it wasn't some esoteric kingdom in the sweet by and by. Nor was it often a kingdom built on the threat of hellfire and brimstone.

For Jesus, the realm of God was not peopled by god and demigods, but instead with everyday people, which meant it was near and it was real. That nearness, and not the threat of eternal agony, was the basis for his call to repentance (*metanoia* or turning around). He transformed human life not by scaring the hell of people, but by helping them see the heaven close at hand.

To be sure, there were times when only brimstone and hellfire seemed to work with the Pharisees or scribes, but there were far more times when his preaching and parables emphasized God's presence in every breathing, waking moment of creation.

His was a kingdom of forgiving fathers and well-paid laborers, the realm of God where persistent widows finally got justice and even tax collectors had a place at the table and in heaven. With his words, he envisioned God in every nook and cranny of everyday life, from cleaning the house to plowing a field. With his words, he opened the eyes of a lawyer to see a Samaritan as good and a neighbor as anyone who shows mercy, even if they belong to the wrong people. With his words, he opened the eyes of his disciples to see God in the children they wanted to shoo away and opened the mind of Nicodemus to see God still yearning to give him new life. Over and again in his preaching and teachings, Jesus used words to expand the understanding of who God was and what God was about in this world.

His words reflected the heart of that kingdom. They were words of love, even when they stung. As he looked down on Jerusalem, he wept for the city and cried out, "If you, even you, had only recognized on this day the things that make for peace!" (Luke 19:42). His words challenged his listeners to be more than they thought they could be. "Go, sell your possessions," he said to the rich young man, which was another way of saying "let go of those things that possess *you*." His words made them think—and then think again. "Tell me about this water," the Samaritan woman asks at the well. "What is this bread of life?" the disciples wonder.

Sometimes his words were those of blessing, be it for the poor in spirit or the poor in goods. Sometimes they were words of conflict and confrontation. "You brood of vipers! You white-washed sepulchers!" He never minced words: "You who devour widows' houses and parade around in your long robes." But he also didn't hold back in other ways either: "Father, forgive."

Whether in parable or pointed statement, blessing or confronting, the point of his words was the same—not just to proclaim God's kingdom on earth as it is in heaven, but to create it through his preaching. And through that preaching, to get people to believe it enough to turn their lives around and trust that good news—*now*.

The purpose of our preaching is the same. Somehow through our mere words to help our congregations know that *now*, in our time, the time is fulfilled. Somehow our sermons, like Jesus', must convince people we're not talking about something that happened a long time ago and has a nice message to teach us, like one of Aesop's fables. Like Jesus, we're talking about a living Word at work in the life of this world, in the listener's life and even in the preacher's.

In addition, like Jesus, we don't proclaim the realm of God as some far off future possibility, at the end of all time or of our time. Instead, in Paul Tillich's familiar words, our sermons proclaim that "now and then in ourselves and here and there in our world, there is a new creation."[2] Moreover, like Jesus, we also have the audacity to point to signs of that new creation in this world.

How to Do It? (i.e., Prepare for Preaching)

Get Yourself in the Word and Get the Word in You

"The Word became flesh and lived among us," writes John of Jesus (John 1:14), which is John's mystical way of saying God's Word was in Jesus. But I think the Word was also in Jesus—and Jesus in that Word—not only in a mystical sense, but as it would have been in any faithful Jewish man of his time. He came from a culture that immersed him and every other child in that

Word. "Keep these words that I am commanding you today in your heart," God said to the Hebrew people. "Recite them to your children and talk about them when you are at home and when you are away, when you lie down and when you rise. Bind them as a sign on your hand, fix them as an emblem on your forehead, and write them on the doorposts of your house and on your gates" (Deut. 6:6–9). That's a pretty full immersion.

In teachings, commandments, the history of his people, psalms, and prophets, God's Word had shaped Jesus just as his carpenter father shaped and honed wood in his shop. You can hear the fullness of that Word echo every time he preached.

In Luke's Gospel, Jesus came out of the wilderness and began his ministry by returning to his hometown of Nazareth. He went into the synagogue, opened the scroll, and read from Isaiah. The congregation ooh-ed and ah-ed at how Joseph's son made Scripture come alive. But then Jesus cited other lessons from Scripture. He reminded them, God's chosen, that there were many widows in Elijah's time, but the prophet was sustained only by a Gentile woman, living in the heathen city of Sarepta. He remembered that in the time of Elisha, there were many lepers in Israel, but only one, Naaman, the Syrian, the Arab, was made whole.

Two stories from Scripture that affirmed the kingdom of God went beyond the city limits of Nazareth and beyond the racial and religious limits of its people. Not exactly the Word the congregation wanted to hear, but it was precisely the Word that needed to be said if God's kingdom was to be realized. Jesus preached the *full* Word of God, because he was fully immersed in it.

As preachers, we need to be as fully immersed in the Word and shaped by it as he was. Scripture isn't something we can scan on Saturday morning and pray to God we might have something meaningful to say about it by Sunday. If Jesus had done that in Nazareth, he might have ended the sermon with the Isaiah text and not offered a fuller vision of God's kingdom.

If the words of our sermons are to give life as Jesus' did, then we must be willing to live our lives in that Word. By that I do not mean a life shaped by the reductionist morality that sometimes passes for God's Word in our time. Nor do I advocate a specific way of "living in God's Word," e.g., morning devotionals.

What I do encourage is an ongoing openness to that Word. Having the courage to make room for it in our daily lives and our daily work. Keeping the study and engagement with the Word as central to our ministry, even in the midst of all the other good works (and busy work) that demand attention.

Being delighted by the fact that indeed, there is always "more light and truth to break forth from God's Word."[3]

Only by immersing ourselves in that Word will we begin to know—and trust—its power. An example. A few years ago, we invited former Secretary of the Interior Stewart Udall to speak at United on environmental issues. More than anyone since Theodore Roosevelt, Secretary Udall changed our country's attitudes and policies about the environment. His writings brought conservation issues to the forefront in the 1960s. As interior secretary, he shepherded through Congress the Wild and Scenic River Act, Wilderness Protection Act, and other major legislation.

Mr. Udall grew up in the Church of Jesus Christ of Latter Day Saints in Arizona (a.k.a., Mormon), but at United, we thought he would focus on environmental and other political issues. He surprised all of us, including me. He didn't begin with the upcoming election or the environmental legislation he helped pass. Instead, he told about growing up in the farmhouse in northern Arizona in the early part of last century, and how on every wall of the kitchen, the parlor, and even the bedrooms were framed "samplers," embroidered sayings and pictures done by his mother and sisters. "The Earth is the Lord's" proclaimed one of them. "Heaven and earth are full of your glory" was another.

These "sampler" Bible verses reminded him and his family who truly was God of heaven and earth. Surrounded by those words, Udall said, gave him the passion and commitment he has had for sixty years to care for God's creation and to get this country to care as well.

Immerse yourself in the word of God so you can hear its call in your life. Immerse yourself in it so you can sound that call to others.

Immerse Yourself in That Word So It Can Come Alive for You and the Congregation

Often the Scriptures we use in preaching are so well-known as to be trite. Jesus faced the same problem. The texts he used were layered with centuries of sermons, teachings, Midrash, and interpretation. But he breathed new life into those texts, combining old images with new understandings in the parables, echoing the prophets' words in new contexts, all for the purpose of making God's kingdom real.

Our preaching requires the same. Immerse yourself in the life of Scripture so that Scripture can come alive. Help your congregation touch, taste, smell, hear the realm of God so close at hand. Get them to smell the fresh-turned dirt when the sower goes out to sow. Breathe in the aroma of the fresh-baked bread made by the woman with her bit of yeast. Help your congregation hear the sound of the prodigal father weeping with joy as he clings to his lost son or the bumbling words of the young man trying to get out his well-rehearsed speech. Let them hear the bleating of the sheep and the goats at the Last Judgment and the disbelief in the voices of those who say, "Lord, when did we see *you* and not care?"

Get inside the Scripture and bring it from thousands of years ago into the here and now of your congregation, so they can say "I know that guy" or "I know that feeling," even if you're talking about a first-century Palestinian shepherd or field hands in a vineyard. Frederick Buechner is a master at it. You won't find better portrayals of the biblical characters than in his essays *Telling the Truth: The Gospel as Tragedy, Comedy, and Fairy Tale*. There's middle-age Abraham, packing up the station wagon to follow the call; old Sarah, laughing until her china teeth rattle, tears run down her face, and she stuffs her apron in her mouth to keep the angel from hearing her; and Pilate, the three-pack-a-day smoker who's just quit until he meets the upcountry prophet named Jesus and without thinking, reaches for a filter tip and takes a long drag that makes his head swim.[4]

No matter how many times we have heard a passage of Scripture, there was a time when it was brand new. It still is. Immerse yourself in it so you can preach it that way.

Immerse Yourself in the Word to Have the Courage to Preach It

Getting the Word in himself stood Jesus in good stead. It was the bare Word of Scripture that Jesus used to fend off Satan's temptations in the wilderness. Not only did Jesus know his Bible better than his adversary, but he trusted its power. As preachers, we need to do the same.

The challenge to his authority as a preacher and teacher didn't end once Jesus left the far side of the Jordan. If anything, the work got harder. Mark writes of the start of Jesus' ministry: "After John had been arrested, Jesus came into Galilee" (1:14). He then outlines what Jesus did—proclaimed the Gospel of God, said the kingdom was at hand, and told people to turn around (repent) and believe the Gospel. In short, the same things that got John arrested.

It doesn't take a Santa Fe psychic to figure out that Jesus was headed for trouble, just like John, for preaching that Gospel of God. In Luke, after Jesus read Isaiah and told of God's favor toward a Gentile woman and a Syrian Arab, his hometown congregation wanted to throw him off a cliff. The Pharisees were always angry with him, whether for healing on the Sabbath or eating with the wrong people; the Sadducees always trying to trick him; and Herod and his henchmen always lurking in the background. Sometimes he got into trouble over petty things, like Martha's being upset at her sister not helping in the kitchen.

If Jesus was fully human, as the Scriptures say and I believe he was, then the temptation to give into fear, doubt, or just a desire to please and not cause waves must have been a constant companion for him—just as it was for the prophets before him and as it is for the rest of us human preachers now.

Throughout his ministry, the word of Scripture gave Jesus what he needed to face such troubles and remain true to his call to proclaim the kingdom of God. Even on the cross, it was Scripture that gave voice to his sorrow: "My God, my God, why have you forsaken me?" (Mark 15:34)

That Word will stand us in good stead in our wildernesses as well, especially the wilderness of preaching. As Tony Robinson writes, "Preaching requires courage because it asks preachers to be servants of the Word, and not servants of the congregation." He continues, "The transforming Word of God is not safe, nor is it comfortable. It is intrusive and threatening."[5] That word can make people as uncomfortable in our time as it did in Jesus. And it can get us into almost as much trouble.

Like Jesus, we can be tempted by all manner of things, from puffed-up pride to wanting to please the crowds to losing the courage of our convictions. Like him, get that Word of God in your bones. Not so you can win the proof-texting game, but so that the people, questions, and dilemmas of those ancient times can be as real to you as the ones you face everyday. Immerse yourself in Scripture so its ancient faith and hope can give you faith and hope now, even before you seek to offer such to your congregation.

Get into the World and Get the World into You

"A sermon," observes the old preacher in Marilynn Robinson's *Gilead*, "is one side of a passionate conversation."[6] I agree with the passion part, but I think the conversation is multisided. Good preaching comes from an ongoing engagement—with God, Scripture, the people we serve, the wider world, those who have studied the texts before us, and with our own lives, present and past.

Again, that's modeled in Jesus' life and preaching. When he was twelve, his parents found him in the Temple, talking with the elders. Throughout his ministry, his disciples, the women, and countless others continually engaged him in conversation. Sometimes the discussions were deep and profound:

"Teach us to pray." "What must I do to inherit eternal life?" Sometime it was the everyday conversation of life together: "How are we going to feed all those people?" And sometimes it was downright petty: "Who's the greatest?" "Tell my sister to help me in the kitchen."

But even the petty questions, like Zebedee's wife asking that her two sons sit closest to Jesus, he often answered with Scripture, opening it up, using the question as an opportunity to explore a deeper truth.

Jesus didn't limit his conversations to his followers or those who agreed with him. He and the Pharisees and Saducees went at it over everything from Caesar's taxes to which of seven brothers get the widow in Paradise. There is nothing like talking with people who disagree with you to teach you what you really believe.

Sometimes even Jesus learned something new. A Canaanite woman came to him, seeking healing for daughter. "Don't throw the children's bread to the dogs," he told her, echoing old teachings about the children of Israel and old prejudices against Gentiles. "True, sir," she countered, "but even the dogs eat the scraps." "What faith you have!" he exclaimed. It takes one heck of a preacher to be that open to new ideas.

Jesus was as immersed with the people of God as with the Word of God. His teaching and preaching arose from the life of the community. He was no guru dispensing wisdom from a mountaintop nor a celebrity preacher shielded from the riffraff by his handlers. Instead he was in the thick of life, listening to people's questions, responding to particular situations, engaging not just his disciples but all kinds of people.

Karl Barth said that the preacher should hold the Bible in one hand and the newspaper in the other, a way to bring the Word and the world into the pulpit. I agree, but I'd also hold my car keys, as a reminder to get out into the homes, offices, schools, and businesses of the people I serve so I can, like Jesus, hear their questions and listen to their lives.

Get Out of Dodge

Or Santa Fe or Omaha or Decatur or wherever God has called you. If you can't do it literally, at least do it figuratively. Jesus went to "lonely places" to pray. We need to do the same, regularly. Otherwise, there's no way to listen either to God or to our lives, both of which are needed for good preaching. Francis of Assisi said, "The preacher must first draw from secret prayers what he will later pour out in holy sermons; he must first grow hot within before he speaks words that are in themselves cold."[7]

Lord knows, I know that's easier said than done, for all kinds of reasons. But do it. As Roger Repohl writes, "Silence allows the word of God to take root in the heart and to transform it. It makes space for hearing things that would not otherwise be audible. . . . Keeping silent is the most productive way to waste time."[8]

If you're a lay leader reading this book, convince the powers that be in your church to support your minister having that time and space. If you're a minister, take it from one who knows—take that time and make that space. It will make you a better preacher.

And if the congregation balks at the idea, ask them what would Jesus do and then point them to the Gospels.

Walk with the Word

It may sound mundane, but I think one reason Jesus was so in touch with both God and the world, and why he could tell such great stories, was that he had to walk so much. You couldn't get from Nazareth to Capernaum to Galilee to Jerusalem without hoofing it, which meant lots of time to consider the lilies of the field and the lives of the people along the way.

Going for a walk is one of the best ways to clear your head and also get inside a Scripture passage. You can play more with the text or take on different character. It's easier to consider a passage from different perspectives if you're literally changing your perspective in a good walk, rather than sitting hunched at your desk. Walking can help break out of the binds we sometimes find ourselves in, be it the paralysis of fear ("You can't say *that*, can you?") or the panic at our own procrastination. Preaching is a physical activity and "walking a sermon" keeps that in mind. Finally walking—or running, playing basketball, hiking, or doing weights—builds strength. We need all we can get to preach honest and faithful sermons.

Read—and Not Just Scripture

I don't know if Jesus did this, but it's important that we do. Read Scripture, but also read the news. Read essays and magazine articles to know what other people are thinking and regard as important. Read articles by people you don't agree with. Most of all, read good stories, fiction and nonfiction. I once heard that Fred Craddock reads a short story every day. Short fiction teaches things we need to know as preachers, from the economy of words to how to make a character real with one small detail. Frederick Buechner read all the *Wizard of Oz* books at an early age, as well as Shakespeare, and you can hear the elegance of the latter and the mystery of the former in every one of his sermons.

Read poetry, be it Emily Dickinson, Mary Oliver, or the latest from your local high school's poetry slam. Like short story writers, poets know how to make a point with a paucity of words. Like the prophets, they also know how to combine words to create new vision.

How to Deliver It? Whatever Way Works

When I came to United, I used a manuscript and preached from behind the small lectern. Gradually I began to step out in front of the Communion table and preached without notes. That wasn't a theological statement, but simply a response to practical issues:

1. The size of the sanctuary. Standing behind a pulpit with sixty people in the congregation seemed artificial.
2. Leading two services that are identical in Scripture and sermon, but with a different feel. Preaching without a manuscript gave me more flexibility in both the content and style of the delivery.
3. Being caught between following the manuscript and wanting to engage the congregation.
4. Mrs. Shields being my 4-H leader, who always told me to look at the audience, not my notes.

The sanctuary and congregation are now considerably larger, but I still preach in front of the Communion table, without notes or a manuscript. It allows me both to engage and gauge the congregation better. I can see if the pace needs to pick up or if I should leave out a story I'd included in the manuscript. (Having 150 editors every Sunday does keep a sermon lively and concise). Bottom line, delivering the sermon without notes lets it be that "passionate conversation" with God and with the congregation.

However, I do write a manuscript, take it into the service with me, and often take one quick look during the hymn before the sermon. But I leave it behind when I stand up to preach.

Why bother writing a manuscript if I don't use it? Because it makes me write my way to new ideas and insights. It gives me a chance to think through phrases and sentences and pay attention to the poetry of the words. Finally and most importantly, it makes certain, before I stand in front of the congregation, that I have actually written to the end of the sermon. ("Keep digging, there's got to be an Amen in there somewhere!") It keeps me honest and makes me do my homework.

Preaching without notes, with or without having prepared a full manuscript, is not for everyone. For one, not everyone had a Mrs. Shields as a 4-H leader. Two, your sanctuary may not lend itself to that style. Three and most importantly, there are a lot of excellent preachers who stand behind the pulpit, preach from a manuscript, and make the Word come alive every Sunday.

Nor is preaching without notes or in front of the pulpit the right approach for every situation. I use the pulpit to conduct funerals because I need the power and presence it symbolizes to hold the community in grief. I also use a manuscript, because I can't trust my memory when I'm trying to be responsive to the family and other mourners.

Preaching without notes is not necessarily the best way for the Word to be offered. It's simply the way that works for me in the setting I'm in. Moreover, like many other decisions in worship, the "technique" (e.g., pulpit or no pulpit, notes or no notes) shouldn't be the criteria for good preaching.

So what are those criteria? Here's what I look for in sermons, be they my own or others:

- Has the preacher done her homework, both in terms of study and also prayer?
- Has he followed St. Francis's teaching to "find the fire in one's own soul"?
- Has the preacher listened deeply to the biblical text, both the text for the day and the Word as a whole?
- Has she listened deeply to the lives of the people she serves and the wider community and world?
- Has the preacher, as Frederick Buechner urges, also listened to his own life?
- Does the sermon make the kingdom of God real and at hand? Is there a sense of urgency —or did the person just "phone it in"?
- Does the sermon honor the "immortal, invisible God only wise" and the everyday lives of the people?
- Does it strengthen their faith—in God, in themselves, in the life of their church, in this world?
- Does it offer deep-rooted hope?
- Will the congregation, individually and as a community, be different—even transformed—because of the sermon?

And one last criterion . . .

• Does it make you want to sit up and take notes?

If the preacher can answer affirmatively to most of the above, then whether they stand in front of the pulpit or behind it or stand on their heads to deliver it, the sermon has done what it is supposed to do—proclaim the lively, challenging, life-changing Word of God and create with their own mere words an encounter with God's kingdom, here and now.

Seven

Bread, Water, and Infinity: The Sacraments

i thank You God for most this amazing
day: for the leaping greenly spirits of trees
and a blue true dream of sky; and for everything
which is natural which is infinite which is yes

(i who have died am alive again today,
and this is the sun's birthday; this is the birth
day of life and of love and wings: and of gay
great happening illimitably earth)

how should tasting touching hearing seeing
breathing any—lifted from the no
of all nothing—human merely being
doubt unimaginable You?

(now the ears of my ears awake and
now the eyes of my eyes are opened)

—e. e. cummings[1]

A **few days into the river trip, it was my turn to help with dinner.** After an hour of unpacking the kitchen boxes, cutting up vegetables, and heating cans of beans, we were ready to serve. The group was scattered along the riverbank, some taking pictures, some reading, others sitting to watch the colors of the water as it flowed by. I called out, "Dinner's in five minutes!"

Then I looked around at the canyon walls and the layers of the earth that surrounded us, and added, "Of course, we're in the middle of rock that's five hundred million years old, but dinner's still in five minutes!"

Dinner in five minutes amidst rock that's millions of years old. That's a good place to begin this chapter on the sacraments and other rituals—those sacred acts and moments in worship when we pour tap water on a baby's head and say it is the water of new life or pass cubes of Wonder Bread and proclaim them to be the bread of life and the body of Christ. In the Christian church, baptism, Communion, and rites like confirmation use texts and practices that are thousands of years old to connect people here and now to the eternal presence and love of God, the infinite, "unimaginable You" of cummings's poem.[2]

We engage in these acts because, despite what I said in the previous chapter about their power, words have their limits. Sometimes rather than talking about something, we need to, as the Nike ad says, "just do it!" The sacraments do what words can't, namely make flesh God's word of love in our lives.

A friend described the first time he kissed his wife. "We started out as friends hanging out together, talking about all kinds of things. Then I realized I was falling in love with her. I wanted her to know that so I told her I thought she was pretty . . . and smart . . . and funny." He paused for a moment. "Then one day when we were talking, I couldn't stand it any longer. I just had to up and kiss her!"

That's a good description of the sacraments. Webster's Dictionary defines a sacrament as "a formal religious act that is sacred as a sign or symbol of a spiritual reality."[3] A traditional definition in the church is "a visible sign of an invisible grace." Perhaps another definition are those times in worship when, whether through the touch of the pastor's hand on our forehead or the taste of bread on our tongue, we let God "just up" and bless us, feed us, heal us.

The sacraments and rites of the church are tangible reminders that God's love for us and for this world knows no limit of time or space. Like a call to supper in the Grand Canyon, they express God's presence in a particular time and place for *all* time—present, past, and future.

When our Jewish brothers and sisters celebrate Passover, they don't just hear about the night their ancestors left Egypt thousands of years ago. They take the journey from slavery to freedom themselves. The unleavened bread, haroseth, and wine, along with the prayers, readings, and songs, remind them not only of long ago when God told Pharaoh, "Let my people go." The living story of Passover also invites them to experience God's liberating presence *now* in their own lives and in the life of this world.

Similarly when we as Christians gather for Communion, we take our place alongside those twelve disciples. Like them, we bring our fears, joys, and hopes to the meal. Hopefully, like them, we will find ourselves welcomed as they were, even if we know only too well how we can betray, deny, and lose our way. We receive bread for our journey and the reminder, in Jesus' words about the new covenant and the realm of God, that God always goes ahead of us, even as God remains present with us.

Baptism also connects us with present, past, and future. A baptism takes place on a specific day at a specified time in the service. Nervous new parents stand before the congregation, holding their baby and hoping he doesn't cry, while the pastor prays to remember his full name, and the people crane their necks to see this new bundle of life and say "yes" to the pastor's questions about caring for this child and all God's children.

But this particular moment of baptism also stretches back to when John the Baptist stood knee deep in the cold waters of Jordan and cried for people to repent or to when the unnamed woman poured her priceless oil over Jesus' head and the fragrance filled the room. It stretches ahead to a future when those parents, no longer new, must rouse their now surly teenager out of bed and into the car for church; when the church must make good on its promises to guide and love that child through those years; and when the child, now grown, may need a reminder in his life that even if he doesn't make the soccer team or his lover walks out or life simply doesn't turn out as planned or hoped, he is still beloved of God and belongs to God.

Indeed that moment extends into God's eternal time. It symbolizes God's promise that when this little baby who cries at the cold waters of baptism crosses the equally cold waters of Jordan in his final journey, he will be met on the other side by the One who blesses him today.

As a "sign of a spiritual reality," the sacraments identify who and what we believe that spiritual reality to be. Be it with water or bread, both sacraments proclaim God as the source of all life. The stories we tell about that water or that bread further name God as the One who conquers death and brings new life; the One who brought the Hebrew people through the waters of the Red Sea and delivered Jonah from the belly of the whale; the One who overcame the fear and betrayal of that last night with love and sacrifice.

The sacraments can also help us see God at work not only in the sacred space and time of worship, but in the world all around us, as the poet cummings said, in "everything which is natural which is infinite which is yes."[4] If we can experience as sacred the Communion meal of bread and cup, then perhaps we can experience as sacred *every* meal, be it a family supper or a quick bite from a fast-food place. If in sharing the Last Supper we can believe God was present that night of betrayal and death, then maybe we can believe God is present even in our times of betrayal and death.

Finally, the sacraments can also help us see ourselves in a new way. Both baptism and Communion identify us as a people who are connected to and claimed by the spiritual reality we call God. They name us as a people who believe in a living God, engaged in human life here and now, and who also believe that God has a claim on our lives. The new life symbolized in the waters of baptism is not a life to be lived solely unto ourselves, but a life of discipleship lived for the sake of others. The broken bread of Communion is a tangible reminder of the sacrificial love that God both offers *to* us and asks *from* us.

In the Christian church, we don't just "perform" the sacraments or "do" the sacraments. We *celebrate* them. The verb implies they are (a) full of life, (b) joyous, and (c) important. The following are some suggestions for how to do that celebration.

"Child of Blessing, Child of Promise, Baptized with the Spirit's Sign"[5]

Take Time to Prepare the Parents or the Adult Candidate

Whether for an adult or an infant, baptism is a rite of passage that can be a profound teaching moment. For parents, as for an adult candidate, it's an opportunity to consider where they are on their own journey of faith—and what they will need to do and what they need from the church to keep the promises they're making.

I try to meet with parents or adult candidates twice before the baptism. In the first session, we go over what baptism is—and isn't. This is especially important if they come from a tradition where baptism is the way to keep from going to hell. The baptism section of the United Church of Christ's "Leader's Box" is a good resource for that conversation. Another is the baptismal prayer from the *Book of Worship* that traces the symbol of water from God's Spirit moving over the face of the deep to Jesus being nurtured in the waters of Mary's womb and being baptized at the River Jordan.

I also give them a copy of the baptismal questions from the *Book of Worship*, and ask them before the next meeting to write down what saying "yes" to those questions means to them. (I incorporate a similar exercise in premarital or precovenantal counseling sessions—i.e., asking a couple to reflect on paper what it will take to "love, honor, and cherish" the other.) Asking the candidate or the parents to write their responses to the baptismal questions makes the vows more than a perfunctory "With God's help, I do."

The prebaptism meetings are also an opportunity to expand the parents' understanding of God's relationship with them and their child. No matter how joyous and delicious was the act of creating the child, the parents were not its ultimate Creator. Their child's everlasting bond is with God, not them. Baptism is an acknowledgement that their child has a soul separate from theirs and that they have a responsibility to nurture that soul.

It's also a chance to support parents in caring for their own souls. By the time they meet with me, the chances are good they already know how demanding and draining this innocent new life can be. Just as baptism is a sign that the child is beloved of God, the parents are equally beloved, and will continue to be so, even when this new beautiful infant pushes every button, drains all patience, and exposes every shadow of anger and frustration in them. In baptism they will hear the promises of the congregation to love and pray not only for their child, but also for them in their new ministry as parents.

With adult candidates, I also underscore what they need to keep their vows, namely their ongoing participation in the community of disciples. The day of baptism is not the end of their journey, but a new beginning to become the people they vow to be.

Finally, use the interest in baptism as an opportunity to guide parents and adult candidates into specific ways of affirming their vows, perhaps in a group focused on the ministry of parenthood, a Bible study, or mission projects.

Connect Infant Baptism to Confirmation

For the first three hundred years of the Christian church, baptism was predominately an adult affair. As such, confirming one's faith was simply part of the sacrament. So too was affirming the candidate's call to ministry as a new disciple.

With the advent of infant baptism, confirmation and commissioning were split from the sacrament. Therefore, if infant baptism is the practice, it's our responsibility to reconnect the parts. Both in the preparatory meetings and in the service itself, emphasize to the parents that their vows stretch all the way to the day of confirmation, fourteen or fifteen years in the future. Likewise, in the questions for the congregation, include one about their commitment to provide a quality confirmation ministry for that child and others in the years to come.

Incorporate Baptism into the Regular Sunday Service

It dispels the notion that baptism is a magical ritual to get "fixed so you won't burn" as a parent once said. It reinforces the understanding that baptism, like all worship, is a communal event. The parents or adult candidates make their promises not just to me as the pastor, but in the presence of a whole lot of people. It is the church that baptizes, not the minister or the family. As Will Willimon states:

> In baptism the church is saying to the candidate [or the parents]: "You must never again think of yourself as 'on your own.' You are ours and we are God's. As we claim you and as God claims you through us, so also your new brothers and sisters will make claims upon you. You are now a part of the Body."[6]

In turn, incorporating baptism into regular worship underscores the church's responsibility to support the candidates, to pray for them and love them "as together we grow in the service and love of God." Finally, it is an opportunity for the congregation to renew its covenant to care not only for the new baby before them, but for *all* of God's children, in the church and in the world, no matter how old.

Even If You Don't Dunk, Make It Tangible

Dip your hand in the water, let it splash through your fingers, pray a blessing over it, and pour it over the baptized's head. Have the Deacons, Congregational Care Team, or Church Council lay hands on the candidate or the parents and godparents during the prayer.

At Jesus' baptism, the heavens opened, the Spirit descended like a dove, and the voice of God said, "This is my Beloved." You may not be able to manage those special effects, but do what ever you can to celebrate the incarnate sign of blessing and new life that baptism is.

Most of all, baptize like you believe it makes a difference. A number of years ago, I baptized the children of a family who had been coming to United for a short time. The parents seemed eager to get involved. We met twice, talked a lot about values and discipleship, and even rehearsed the baptism. Both parents enthusiastically answered "I do, with the help of God" when I asked them to offer their children the love and nurture of the Christian church and serve as role models in their own lives and faith. I was impressed by their commitment.

Four months later, the parents went through a messy, angry divorce. I never saw either of them nor the children again. It was hard not to feel like a sucker.

A year or so ago, I answered the phone at the church and heard a young woman's voice I didn't recognize. She said, "You probably don't remember but you baptized me and my brother when we were kids. I'm getting married, and I was wondering if you would do the service." She explained that after her parents' divorce, neither of them would take her to church anywhere. She had gone through a troubled time of addiction, but had been clean and sober for several years. So had her fiancé. "United's my church home," she said, "because that's where I was baptized. I still remember everyone singing and the feel of the water on my head. I want to reconnect. Will you do my wedding?" "I would be honored," I told her.

Baptize like you believe it makes a difference. Because it does.

The Joyful Feast of the People of God

"The first Sunday of the month was Communion Sunday at Emmanuel A.M.E Church in Charleston, South Carolina," Reuben Sheares used to tell. "The congregation would come forward for Communion while the choir sang from the balcony. After the people had finished, the choir stopped singing and came down the stairs to the front."

"As they filed in," Reuben continued, "a little man sitting off to the side would stand and raise up a song:

> Bye and bye, when the morning comes,
> All the saints of God come gathering home.
> We will tell the story how we overcome,
> And we'll understand it better, bye and bye.[7]

"The whole congregation would join in,' Reuben said, "singing just that chorus over and again until all had communed.

"That man was my daddy," he continued. "It was the only song I ever heard him sing, the first Sunday of every month, Communion Sunday at Emmanuel A.M.E. Church in Charleston, South Carolina.

"It was a song that could sing itself," he said. "A song that a young Black man growing up at that time in South Carolina knew he needed to sing."[8]

"Bye and bye, when the morning comes . . ." The song also reminds us what to keep in mind whenever we celebrate the sacrament of Communion.

"When the Morning Comes . . ."

"This is the joyful feast of the people of God!" proclaims the invitation to the table. There is certainly an irony in that invitation. After all, the meal leads into a night of betrayal and death. But its final destination is Easter dawn.

Communion proclaims that morning still comes. However you celebrate Communion in your congregation, make it joyful. I'm not talking about mere happiness or satisfaction, but true joy. Joy that's been around the block. Joy that is sometimes born in sorrow, joy that often follows difficult nights of the soul, but that *will* come in the morning.

Communion is an honest celebration. It recognizes the power of fear and hatred, but also proclaims that the power of God's love is greater. When the early Christians celebrated Communion, they did so not only to look back and remember the Last Supper, but also to rejoice in the presence of the Resurrected One in their meal and in their midst. We need to do the same.

Making Communion joyful doesn't always mean spirited celebration with lots of music, though it often does. But the joy of Communion is rooted in the experience of God's presence in all times, even the hardest. It can be known equally in the solemnity of Maundy Thursday or the rambunctiousness of a Mardi Gras Sunday. It's no accident that the Communion section of *The New Century Hymnal* includes both the mysterious and brooding "Let All Mortal Flesh Keep Silent" and the jazzy, Jamaican "Let Us Talents and Tongues Employ." Both hymns proclaim in distinct ways that Communion "*is* the joyful feast of the people of God."[9]

To underscore the movement of Communion from fear to joy, night to dawn, don't just tack it on to the end of the service once a month or a quarter. When you celebrate it, build the rest of the service—sermon, prayers, songs—around it. Let everything in the service lead up to Communion, so it can indeed be the joyful and powerful response to God's word and presence.

"All the Saints of God Come Gathering Home . . ."

However you celebrate this feast, make it inclusive. The first Communion was. The disciples came from different backgrounds and held dramatically different beliefs about Jesus Christ. One person at that table would betray him, another would deny him, and all the rest would flee away. Yet every one of them shared the meal. If Jesus could welcome all of them, certainly we can welcome all to the table as well.

Moreover, in the United Church of Christ, we have the freedom to extend that welcome in ways many other traditions don't. In a time when religious divisions, along with political, economic, gender, and racial differences, are often a cause for violence, being able to welcome all people to the table is a powerful gift—and responsibility.

Make sure that your practice of Communion embodies the words you say about it. We may proclaim "God's radical welcome," but if we gather in a tight circle around the table, new people may not experience it that way. A church may claim to be inclusive, but if I'm a recovering alcoholic and I don't know if it's wine or grape juice in that cup, I'm not going to risk finding out. The minister may proclaim it's an abundant feast with enough all, but if the servers are stingy with the bread, we might not believe it.

If you're the celebrant, memorize the words of liturgy so you can look at the congregation as you tell the story and invite them to the table. Proclaiming God's welcome with your nose buried in your worship book sends a mixed message.

In the liturgy, include not only the congregation, but also the world. Sometimes at United the invitation connects the celebration of Communion with other meals and also with the persons we serve in our outreach ministries. Here is a part of a Communion litany that expresses that connection:

In many and various ways, God offers us the bread of life—in our families and circles of friends, in school cafeterias and over business lunches, in church potlucks and in this sacred meal of bread and cup.

May this meal remind us how God blesses us with food and life every day.

In many and various ways, God also calls us to share our bread with others.

May this meal remind us of our brothers and sisters who are guests at the Youth Shelter and who gather in their kitchens of Habitat Houses.

In this meal, God also calls us to remember those who have no bread,

And may this Communion strengthen our commitment to share our bread and the love of this community with our brothers and sisters.

Communion can connect us with the wider community in other ways, too. The repetition of the Communion story and liturgy provides an opportunity to incorporate simple phrases in languages other than the dominant language of the congregation. At United, using Spanish terms such as *gracias a Dios, il pane da vida* (the bread of life), or *il cuerpo di Cristo* (the body of Christ) is a reminder of "all the saints who come gathering home." It also reminds us that God is bilingual, even if we're not.

"We Will Tell the Story How We Overcome . . ."

I believe our commitment to the radically inclusive nature of Communion includes even the different beliefs people have about the sacrament. On any given Sunday, when I stand behind the table, I look out on a congregation of people as varied in their understandings of what Communion means as they are in every other aspect of their lives. For some, the meal is simply a re-enactment of the Last Supper, a memorial meal. For others, it is *the* symbol of God's victory over death, not only "bye and bye" but here and now.

For some, the bread and cup become the transubstantiated body and blood of Jesus Christ. For others, the elements represent our common need for bread, and through that, our common need for God. For still others, the importance of the meal is that all are welcome to the table. Finally, there are those who say "yes" to all of the above, and others who come forward because that's what everyone else is doing.

As I tell new people in our "What is the United Church?" sessions, Communion is the coming together of all those experiences of the story we tell at the table. As a celebrant, my job is to tell that story, welcome everybody to the meal, pray for God's transforming and life-giving Spirit, and make sure everyone gets fed. Neither I nor other worship leaders are the "Communion police," making sure everyone has the right doctrine about the sacrament.

How an individual interprets the sacrament of Communion is up to them. How they get fed and transformed by it is up to God.

Similarly, there is no one "right" way to celebrate Communion. Some congregations come forward to receive, others stay seated. Some use a common loaf, others bread cubes. Some drink, others use intinction (dipping the bread into the cup). Other churches pass plates with wafers and trays with individual glasses. I personally like the movement of people coming forward to share from a common loaf and common cup. But as the story about Tom in chapter 3 illustrates, other methods of sharing communion can have equally great meaning.

The issue isn't so much how we celebrate Communion, but that we do it well, with meaning and depth. We may say it is a sacrament, but if we're careless or sloppy in how we lead it, if the Deacons or servers don't know what they're supposed to do, or if it looks like "Keystone Cops do church," our congregations can rightly question how holy and important we really think Communion is. Take time to walk through the service with your Deacons or servers. Practice your part, too.

"And We'll Understand It Better Bye and Bye"

This joyful feast represents the very core of the Christian faith. Whether we sit in the pews or come forward, kneel at a rail or pass a tray, we are participating in an act that we believe Jesus himself did and told us to do: breaking bread and sharing the cup.

In that sharing, Communion proclaims, in the words of Martin Luther King Jr., "Our God is able." Able to turn the worst we humans can do into something good. Able to overcome fear, hatred, and even death itself.

It even proclaims, as they sang at Emmanuel A.M.E. Church in Charleston, South Carolina, that God is able to make *us* able to overcome whatever fear or prejudice or hurt this world sends our way.

This joyful feast is a mighty powerful meal. Make sure your congregation knows that.

Eight

"Sing Alleluia . . . and Keep on Walking": Music in Worship

Mountains of music swell in the river, hills of music billow in the creeks . . . while other melodies are heard in the gorges of the inner canyons. The Grand Canyon is a land of song.

—John Wesley Powell[1]

or eighteen days, the sound of the river was our constant companion. As Powell experienced, it swelled, billowed, and flowed all around us. The sound roared as we approached rapids. In still waters, the river flowed almost silently through the canyon. At night, as I slept on the raft, the sound enveloped me in the darkness. More than anything else, I missed that sound when the trip was over. It felt like the sound of life itself.

"The Christian liturgy was born singing," Joseph Gilineau wrote, "and it has never ceased to sing."[2] When pregnant old Elizabeth greeted her pregnant young cousin, Mary threw back her head and sang, "My soul magnifies the Lord, and my spirit rejoices in God my Savior." (Luke 1:47) When the angel announced to the shepherds the birth of that child, a heavenly chorus joined in the news. When the Jerusalem crowds heralded Jesus' entrance, they sang an ancient psalm of Hosanna. On the last night of his life, after he had shared the meal with his disciples, they all "sang a hymn and went out" to Gethsemane. The next day, the chances are good the women who witnessed his death raised their lamentations and keened their sorrow.

Imprisoned in Philippi, Paul and Silas sang their praise to God. Throughout his Revelation, John of Patmos saw, and heard, multitudes of elders and saints singing their Hallelujah Choruses to the Lamb.

The Christian church has kept singing for two thousand years. Even Augustine, not known for his poetic nature, knew the power and importance of music in the Christian faith:

> So brothers and sisters, let us sing "Alleluia" now. Let us sing as travelers along the road, but keep on walking . . . So sing "Alleluia" and keep on walking.[3.]

As a preacher, I probably shouldn't confess this, but there are Sundays I am more grateful than usual for Isaac Watts, Charles Wesley, Ruth Duck, Andre Crouch, Natalie Sleeth, Pablo Sosas, and other composers whose names I can't remember. I'm equally grateful for the pianists, organists, guitar players, choir directors, and singers who make their music come alive. When I doubt the sermon will speak to anyone, I know they will be fed by the music.

Even on "good" Sundays, I am still grateful for—and humbled by—the gift of music in worship. In ways not even science can fully explain, music connects with the deepest part of our souls. Its rhythm and rhymes are often the earliest things we can remember, which is why preschoolers memorize their ABCs in song and advertisers come up with catchy jingles. Music is often the last thing we forget. I've visited persons in nursing homes who can't remember my name or that of their spouses or children, but still know "Silent Night" by heart.

Music can take us out of our everyday lives of paying bills, earning a living, and chauffeuring kids, and immerse us in an experience of the eternal. Not only does it express our praise and longing for God, but it gives us an *experience* of God's divine beauty and pathos.

By turning our attention to God, music fulfills an important pastoral, as well as priestly and liturgical, role in worship. Pastoral care is often seen as visitation or individual counseling, focused on personal feelings or immediate needs. But as Thomas Troeger affirms, sometimes "we can be more helpful by providing resources (like music) for renewal which their feelings have blocked from view." Troeger recalls:

A day when I went to worship . . . and was obsessed with a problem that I had turned around and around in my mind. At every turn it had the same unsolvable appearance. Then we sang the opening hymn:

Immortal, invisible, God only wise,
in light inaccessible hid from our eyes,
most blessed, most glorious, the Ancient of Days,
almighty, victorious, thy great name we praise.

The melodic outline of the major triads that open the hymn combined with those great words of wonder, "Immortal, invisible," snapped something loose in my soul. I was no longer circling around and around the same problem. I was swept into a state of prayer from which I later returned with fresh energy to address the situation.

The church offered pastoral care, Troeger concludes, "*not* by asking me what I was feeling or what I wanted but by directing me to the chief end of all human existence: the praise of God."[4]

Music plays an equally important role in the work for justice and peace. By connecting us to the Ultimate and to one another, music can give us the courage and strength we need to persevere in that work. During the civil rights movement, before they went out to face the police dogs and water cannons, African Americans gathered in churches to pray, listen to sermons, and especially sing. In "Amandla: A Revolution in Four-Part Harmony," filmmaker Lee Hirsch documents the power of music of the struggle against apartheid in South Africa. "The thing that saved us was music," affirmed one activist, "it was part of liberating ourselves."[5] Hirsch also notes the relationship between the anti-apartheid resistance and the music. "The struggle gave birth to that specific type of song, songs of resistance," he states. "But I think at a certain point it probably switched, that the songs were bringing whole new groups of people into the struggle."[6] The music arose from the resistance and also gave people the courage to join the resistance.

We saw music's power to give hope and courage in the aftermath of September 11, 2001, when people across the country poured into churches, synagogues, and mosques. What they wanted most, it seemed, was music. The hunger to be together and especially to sing together was palpable, even for people who hadn't set foot in a church in years. In that tragic time, the music of the church was indeed a way "to calm our fears and bid our sorrows cease."

New research in neuropsychology provides insight into the transforming power of music, both individually and for communities. In the therapeutic technique EMDR (Eye Movement Desensitization and Reprocessing), used for trauma recovery, the client recalls the original traumatic event and the fears it triggered. Then they identify a "preferred positive belief" about themselves. Through either visual or auditory cues (eye movement, tapping, etc.), the belief is reinforced, letting the new information replace the old.

Music does the same in worship, whether we're singing an age-old hymn or a new praise song, listening to a solo piano piece, or tapping our foot to sacred jazz. Through word and sound, music can replace our old information of despair or hurt we bring to worship with God's new information of hope, faith, and love for us and for our world.

As much as any sermon, music is a primary expression of our theology. Through its words, style, and presentation, music tells us about the God we seek to worship and the people we seek to be.

It also identifies us, individually and as congregations. Hymns and other songs remind us of our past, of cherished loved ones or special times in our lives or the life of our church. They can also remind us of God's love for our particular communities or cultures, even if the wider world doesn't. Carol Doran and Thomas Troeger tell of a Native American woman who learned that a new denominational hymnal included one of her people's favorite hymns. "I never believed," she said to the hymnal editor, "that I would live to see the day when you would count the songs of my people worthy of your singing."[7]

Connection with the Ultimate, courage in the struggle for justice and peace, identity, expression of our deepest yearnings and our highest praise, the first thing we learn and the last we forget. That's the power of music in our lives and our communities. If it's not vital, then neither our worship nor our congregations will be.

So what makes music vital? The answer(s) would easily fill another book in this series. Here are some things I try to keep in mind.

Hear Things Whole

From prelude to postlude, gatherings songs to sending out music, each individual piece of music in worship is part of an arc that stretches from beginning to end in each service. Whether you are the music director, the minister, or part of the Worship Team, "hear things whole." As one member of United said, "Think opera—or the movies."

In choosing music, consider how the individual selections (prelude, children's song, anthem, hymns) connect to the overall theme of the service. Also, how do they enable the congregation to do what they came to do—i.e., gather in God's presence, prepare, experience, and respond to that presence?

In more liturgical traditions like Catholic or Lutheran, the musical shape of the traditional sung Mass provides the framework for the service, moving from the petition of the opening *Kyrie* (Lord, have mercy) to the praise of the *Gloria*, the response of the creed after the sermon, and the final *Dona Nobis Pacem* that both calls people to the Communion table and sends them out into the world. But even in a "free church" tradition like the United Church of Christ, individual hymns and other music need to have a sense of connection, movement, and purpose in the overall service.

Hearing things whole also means hearing the sound of silence. Any musician can tell you that in music the rests are as important as the notes. The same is true in worship. Even in the most exuberant and joyful service, make time for silence. It's a chance to catch your breath and for God to get a word in.

Be a Congregation, Not an Audience

However you do it, get your congregation singing. It's one of the great gifts of our Protestant heritage. In the Reformation, the music of the church was no longer restricted to the clergy or a choir of men and boys. Instead the whole congregation sang, old and young, male and female, clergy and lay. It brought the community together, gave them hope, and helped them keep the faith. It can do the same for our congregations.

Thanks to technology, there is probably more music available in our time than ever before. Ironically, also thanks to technology, the opportunities for *making* music are decreasing. We can listen to scores of iPod selections and hundreds of radio channels, but outside of church, there aren't many places we're invited to join in. So don't let music be a spectator sport in your congregation.

Take a look at music in your worship service. Is it limited to the traditional format of three hymns, an offertory, prelude, and postlude? How could music enhance the service further? Some congregations start with fifteen minutes of hymn or praise singing to get people warmed up and ready for worship. Others use sung responses to the Psalms or the Gospel readings. Still others use a sung benediction to send people into the world. Adding more music may mean cutting back on other parts of the service, such as the announcements or even the sermon length. As a preacher, I think it's worth it.

Who "does" music in the service? What's the role of the congregation—active participant, listener, audience? Is the music accessible? We may proclaim "Joyful, Joyful" with its call: "Mortals, join the happy chorus!" But if the pitch is too high, most of us won't be able to join in. Are people encouraged to sing? The praise band soloist may be star quality and the guitarist able to do fancy licks, but the congregation is reduced to singing only the chorus in unison.

What's the role of the choir? Along with offering the anthem or offertory, have them help lead the congregation's singing. Even if they sit in a divided chancel, have them face the congregation on the hymns, or better yet, move into the middle to sing and move back as the congregation is being seated.

Be bold and try some congregational hymns in harmony. On the last hymn, have the choir process into the aisles so the congregation can hear the four parts. Teach a simple round, like the Tallis Canon ("Praise God from whom all blessings flow"), to help the congregation hear different voices singing the same song. Singing in harmony might be a stretch for our congregations, but it's a great exercise for learning to *work* together in harmony.

Get all ages to sing—together. Forego the children's sermon, pass out rhythm instruments, and share a song with the children. I guarantee they will remember the experience of making a joyful noise to the Lord with a whole lot of adults far more than any children's sermon.

Find out *all* the musicians in the church and see how you can incorporate them into worship over the course of the year. Not just staff members or choir singers, but also the teenager who plays flute in the high school band or drums in his garage. Perhaps you have members who sing in barbershop groups or the community chorus, children who take piano lessons or play in a youth orchestra. Identifying *all* the musicians in the congregation opens up possibilities for all kinds of sacred music in the life of your church.

Don't confine music only to the worship service, but incorporate it into every part of your church's life. Sing to begin your council meeting and close your congregational gatherings. Sing to say grace at potlucks. Sing songs of justice and peace on mission trips, sing songs of hope and comfort with your Deacons or Congregational Care Team.

Make sure music is a part of your children's and youth ministries. Gone are the days of a piano in every house and music education, particularly choral music, in every school. Gone, too, are the days when the culture did Christian education for us. I learned as many Christmas carols, spirituals, and even songs like "Fairest Lord Jesus" in public school as I did in Sunday school. In our time, if children are to receive the gifts of faith, courage, and hope that music gave many of us, it's up to us to provide it.

In the United Church of Christ, we put great value on people finding their voice for political or social issues. We need to value their musical voices as well.

Get People Talking about Sacred Music

Even if everyone in your congregation comes from the same faith tradition or ethnic or racial background, the music that feeds their souls and expresses their praise of God may differ dramatically. It's important to know (a) what makes music sacred for them, and (b) what are their sacred songs.

How to find that out? Ask them. Get people together, whether as the Church Council, Worship Team, Deacons, Youth Group, or some intergenerational mix, and simply ask, "What is a song that speaks to your soul?" Or "What song connects you to God?" "Tells you about Jesus Christ?" "What music lifts your spirits?" "A song that got you through a long night of your soul?" "Music that gives you courage?" "What music would you want at your funeral—or wedding—or child's baptism?" With all of these questions, ask a follow-up "Why?"

Notice what the questions *don't* ask. They're not "What music do you like?" nor "What should we sing in worship?" Instead they ask what connects us to God and why. They take us out of the realm of personal likes and dislikes and reframe the conversation into one focused on, in Underhill's definition of worship, "the response of the creature to the Eternal."[8]

Their answers don't need to come from the hymnal or even be "official" sacred music. What has offered hope or connected them to God could come from a Broadway musical, like *Carousel's* "You'll Never Walk Alone" or "Seasons of Love" from *Rent*. Maybe it's Aaron Copland's "Appalachian Spring" or the movie score from *Lord of the Rings*, or something sung by Garth Brooks or Crystal Gayle, Bono or Led Zepplin.

Before we hyperventilate about such musical choices, the question is not to recommend the songs for next Sunday, but a way to get people to think "outside the hymnal" about what makes music sacred—i.e., not necessarily its imprimatur from a church, but its ability to open us to the presence of God and the people of God.

In sharing the music that speaks to our souls, we also share our hopes and understandings of God across differences of ages or backgrounds. Listening to a teenager explain why Bono speaks to her of God also tells us what she believes about that God.

As part of the conversation, ask "Why do we include music in worship?" The answers I've heard range from "To glorify God" and "Find hope" to "Be comforted" and "Be challenged" to "Connect us to one another" and "Connect us to people different from us." The diversity can help us understand the different spiritual needs people bring to worship and remind us why we need to sing one another's songs.

Talk about the different faith traditions—and therefore different music traditions—represented in your congregation. Members may come from a variety of different church and unchurched backgrounds. Consequently even their "official" sacred music may well range from Methodist stomps to Gregorian chant, J. S. Bach to Amy Grant.

Listen to what your community—and the world—are singing. What are the musical languages of your town, city, or region? For example, Santa Fe is known for its classical music (the Opera, Desert Chorale, etc.), and we use a good deal in our services. But the region is also home to Mariachi music, Penitente laments, a community band, contemporary dance, and Native American rhythms, many of which have been incorporated into worship at United. Your community probably has an equally rich music tapestry. Should that music be incorporated in your services?

Visit other faith communities to find out what they're doing musically. In Santa Fe, that list would include a Catholic Life Teen Mass, a Pentecostal "shout" service in Spanish for new immigrants, the Greek Orthodox Church's chants, First Presbyterian's weekly organ concerts, and the hard rock service at "The Light." The intent is not necessarily to copy what others are doing, but to know what's in the ears and souls of other Christians. Experiencing the sacred music of other faith communities can also help us understand the depth and breadth of the Christian musical tradition, much like exploring the side canyons on the river trip helped me understand what makes the Grand Canyon grand. And it can help us identify our congregation's particular musical calling.

Move beyond your local community, and perhaps your comfort level, and get a teenager to share their iPod with you to find out what they're listening to. What songs do children learn in preschool? Channel surf your radio and hear the array of voices from country western to classical.

116

I'm not asking us to like any or all of what we hear in the wider world, nor am I advocating incorporating all of it—or any of it—in worship. But to develop vital music for our congregations we need to know the music that is vitally important to many people in the world around us. Only then can we make informed decisions about the music we use in worship and also understand some of the challenges we're up against.

Finally, ask why your church does the music it does. Perhaps your congregation's particular musical tradition is a source of identity, and pride, for your members. It could be what your church is known for in your community, not just musically but theologically.

There may also be some less than stellar reasons. Perhaps your music is what the minister, music director, or another individual wants. Maybe you've "always done it this way." Or perhaps no one has had the time to explore what else might be possible. Whatever the reasons, take time periodically to look at why you do the music you do and see if it still expresses your values and beliefs as a congregation.

Make Music a Priority

To engage in the kinds of conversations outlined above requires an investment of time and energy by the congregation. To make music a priority in worship and education also requires a financial investment. That doesn't necessarily mean the biggest organ or most popular praise band, but it does mean competitive salaries for music staff (in both worship and education) and sufficient funds for instrument maintenance. Our hymns may proclaim "Our God is an Awesome God," but our out-of-tune piano says something else.

Making music a financial priority can be a challenge in many congregations. Just as the arts are the first programs cut in our schools, music is often seen as a dispensable in our churches, especially as we face dwindling membership and rising costs for everything from utilities to health insurance.

In addition, sometimes we can pit the music budget against our commitment to justice and outreach, rather than seeing vital outreach as an outgrowth of vital music and worship. When I started at the church I currently serve, there was no accompanist for the Sunday morning services because "there was no money" due to the difficult transitions of the previous two years. At the same time, the church had committed 10 percent of the budget for outreach giving, including Our Church's Wider Mission (OCWM).

With Reuben Sheares's advice to "keep worship central," I asked if we could cut back on outreach giving for a year just to have the seed money for a

Sunday morning pianist. It didn't fly. As one person stated, "We shouldn't be spending money on ourselves when there was so much need in the world."

But the Southwest conference minister at the time, Rev. Carole Keim, understood the need to strengthen our worship life in order to rebuild the community and our ministry. She recommended that the church reduce its outreach giving, including OCWM, for two years to be able to pay a Sunday pianist.

As the church has grown over the years, due in large part to our vital music and worship, so too has our financial commitment to outreach. The two-year reduction in OCWM that Carole recommended was one of the best investments the conference could have made. She got the connection between worship and mission, and this local church, the wider Santa Fe community, and the wider United Church of Christ benefited from that wisdom.

Strive for Excellence

Music is a gift from God. So too is musical talent. Respect both gifts by setting high standards and being well-rehearsed. Respect the congregation, too. You never know who needs the beauty or pathos of your music to restore their faith—or perhaps just to get through their day.

At the same time, don't confuse excellence with perfection. Unlike *American Idol*, church can be a safe place for children, youth, and even adult musicians to play or sing and know they will be affirmed, even if they make a mistake. Old, young, and in-between, give both God and the congregation your best, and trust that both will be forgiving if you miss a beat.

Contemporary? Traditional? Eternal

How to keep music vital is one question. *What* music is vital to worship is an equally important consideration.

Asking that question can land one on the front lines of the dreaded "worship wars." Because it is so powerful in our lives and faith, music is also the center of most of the arguments about worship. Congregations will often tolerate changes in the liturgy, reading the Scripture in modern English or another language, even bad preaching, but include too many new hymns or introduce instruments other than the organ, and all bets are off.

At the other end of the spectrum, in an effort to attract younger or "unchurched" people, many churches disdain any classical music (i.e., anything written in a previous century by "dead white men") and rely solely on contemporary praise music (generally written by live white men) that is as homogeneous as the popular culture from which it derives. In so doing, they discard music that has given people hope and faith for generations—and still has the power to do so.

But where to begin the conversation? First, get beyond the "traditional" vs. "contemporary" debate. The word "tradition" simply means "handing on," as in Paul writing to the Corinthians "I handed on to you what I received"— the story of Jesus' death and resurrection, the appearances of the risen Christ, and most of all, his own experience of God's grace over and again. Even the most contemporary Christian music is "traditional," since it seeks to hand on the tradition of that good news, albeit with electric guitars and videos.

Likewise, "contemporary" means "marked by characteristics of the present." Even if a worship service doesn't use music written less than one hundred years ago, played on an organ that is even older, and is built with a liturgy that dates back to the fourth century, the service is happening *now*, in present time. The liturgy and the music may seem older than God, but the people engaged in that worship bring to it the cares of this contemporary world and their very present concerns and lives.

If worship is "the response to the Eternal," then the music of our worship needs to have that sense of the Eternal as well. Fact is, Christian sacred music has always blended traditional forms with contemporary styles.

Using the Devil's Tunes for the Lord's Work

Francis of Assisi did it, when he used the love songs of the troubadours to compose, in his native Italian, his love songs to God such as "Cantico della Creature," or "All Creatures of our God, Now Sing."

Bach did it, too. His most famous chorale, "O Sacred Head Now Wounded," was based on a German love song. Handel did it. When opera was banned in eighteenth-century England, the composer incorporated arias and recitatives in his oratorios, including *Messiah*, and got into trouble with the clergy for doing so.

Isaac Watts, John and Charles Wesley, and the other English and American hymn writers of the Great Awakening also did it, turning tunes like the drinking song "The Ballad of Captain Kidd" (with lines such as "God's laws I did forbid, so wickedly I did when I sailed, when I sailed") into sacred songs like "What Wondrous Love Is This."

Thomas Dorsey and Mahalia Jackson also did it, using the rhythms of blues and jazz to develop a new, and controversial, Christian music known as Gospel.

"It" is using "the Devil's songs for the Lord's work," and it's been going on for centuries. As far back as ancient Israel, people of faith have listened to the wider world for inspiration in their sacred song. Even though Yahweh was "a jealous God before whom there should be no others," Carol Doran and Thomas Troeger affirm that "the praise of Yahweh drew upon songs . . . common to many peoples in the ancient Near East, reinterpreting them in the light of the community's faith."[9] Similarly, the choruses of thousands in John's Revelation are Christian versions of Roman spectacles, with the Lamb of God replacing the emperor as the center of praise.

Not surprisingly, the debates about music in worship have been going on for centuries as well. Strong opinions and beliefs about the sounds of worship echo throughout the Bible. "Praise the Lord with clanging cymbals," says the psalmist, "loud clashing cymbals." (Psalm 150:5) And the prophets answer, "I despise your festivals . . . I will not listen to the melody of your harps." (Amos 5:23)

Likewise, "Gross Disorders and barefaced Affronts to common Decency" was one Boston minister's description of the new energetic music by Watts and the Wesley brothers in the Great Awakening.[10] He was describing music such as "O for a Thousand Tongues to Sing" or "Marching to Zion" that is now an established part of the Christian tradition.

So if the plumb line for music in worship isn't "traditional good, contemporary bad" or vice versa, then what is? Here's a question to start the conversation.

What Would Jesus Sing?

The question isn't as flip as it sounds. Exploring the music Jesus sang or heard can both broaden and deepen the conversation about sacred music. As a Jewish child, Jesus would have learned the Psalms from an early age. Those ancient songs are as varied a compilation of music as any contemporary hymnal. Consequently his repertoire would have included personal lamentations, national anthems, quiet reflection, and congregational singing, all developed over centuries of time and diversity of cultures.

We know that Jesus knew such songs, because when he confronted the scribes over doctrine, shared the Last Supper with his disciples, or hung from the cross the next day, it was the Psalms he turned to for hope and courage.

Jesus probably heard or sang other songs, too. Some would have been traditional, like his people's hymns of Passover and Purim and his ancestor Miriam's song of victory in the Exodus. Others were contemporary, such as his mother's canticle of joy, his old uncle Zechariah's song of peace, and everyday folk tunes and children's play songs.

120

Paradoxically Jesus was surprisingly mum about the hows and whats of music. He taught his followers how to pray, fast, give alms, and resolve disputes. But he said not a word about what made music sacred. Perhaps he simply knew it when he heard it.

So what are some criteria for sacred—and vital—music in our congregations? Here are five I use:.

Sacred Music Honors God's Imagination

"Bring Many Names," sings a new hymn by Brian Wren, to tell of our many-faceted God. "Strong mother God, Warm father God, Young growing God, Old aching God, wiser than despair."[11] Of course, no one hymn or piece of music can offer the myriad images we need of God, Jesus Christ, or the Holy Spirit. But the overall musical language of a congregation should strive to offer what songwriter and minister John Bell calls the "full story of faith."

Unfortunately Bell notes, "You can look at much new songwriting . . . since the 1960s and not get a sense that Christ was incarnate. The songs talk a lot about enthroning Jesus in our praises. [But] you never get a Christ that argues, who's angry, who deals with women, who heals people. . . . In the end, these songs are debilitating to the faith."[12]

Not only the text or content, but also the style of music should reflect our faith in the mystery and complexity of God. We may sing "How Great Thou Art" or "Thy Word Is a Lamp unto My Feet," but if our music is from only a single century—whether nineteenth or twenty-first—it portrays a God who either hasn't learned anything new in the last two hundred years or has no sense of history.

As Bell observes, "Congregations that only sing one style of music want only one kind of person. And if you have only one kind of person, you are able to see only one kind of God."[13]

Sacred Music Honors the Human Condition

If all we ever sing is upbeat praise music, we may be unintentionally saying that God is present only in the good times, and not in the times of sorrow or grief. If our music never makes it out of a minor key or feels staid and stuffy, one could rightly wonder if we believe in the goodness of life and the grace of God.

Our music needs to be honest about being human. If God was willing to take on human life in all its sorrow and joy, then our sacred songs should do the same.

121

Sacred Music Helps Us Love Our Neighbor

Loving our neighbor is at the heart of our faith. One way to do that is by singing our neighbor's music, even if it may not be familiar to us or doesn't immediately feed our own souls. And there's never been a better time to sing our neighbor's music than now. In these early years of the twenty-first century, sacred music is definitely global music.

Incorporating the sacred sounds of other cultures, generations, and nations into our church's worship isn't simply an exercise in ethnomusicology. It's part of our mission as a just peace church. Liberation theologian Gustavo Gutierrez writes that Christians "must be concerned not just for the non-believer, but for the non-person."[14] His criteria apply not only to governmental or church policies, but also to our music. Who is not being represented in our sacred song? What cultures, races, classes, or generations are left out?

When we incorporate into worship the music of persons of different backgrounds, languages or cultures, we affirm their status as children of God. From the time I was seven, my family lived in a predominately white middle-class community in Arizona. My elementary school was primarily white. So was my church. But in *The Pilgrim Hymnal* were spirituals like "Were You There?" and "Let Us Break Bread Together." On TV, I heard African Americans singing "We Shall Overcome." The music not only opened my ears, but it opened my eyes, heart, and mind to see a more inclusive vision of God's love and realm than what I saw around me.

If we sing someone's song, we might be able to see them as full human beings, and therefore more willing to pay them a living wage, offer equal housing, or perhaps even choose not to go to war with them.

Sacred Music Acknowledges We're Not the First Generation to Sing Our Faith

In an effort to be modern and especially attract new people, many churches don't just discard classical or traditional sacred music. They deride it. The website of one congregation advertises their contemporary service with the statement: "I like jazz and rock, not hymns and Bach."

Such attitudes are neither helpful nor accurate. Number one, neither hymns nor Bach need to be boring. Number two, Johann Sebastian and jazz have a lot in common. I believe we have a responsibility in the church to help our congregations make that connection and to pass on to coming generations the rich heritage of our Christian musical faith. Why not a website that affirms, "Jazz, rock, *and* J. S. Bach"?

To learn the musical heritage of the church is not a quaint historical inquiry, but a spiritual journey to experience the power of music across time and cultures. But if we don't take that mission seriously, some church leaders and scholars predict we could lose two millenia of Christian music in the next two decades.

Far more than just notes on a page would be lost should that happen. Losing the classical tradition of Christian music would also mean losing our connection with the faithful women and men of generations who sang their souls through such music. It also means losing the depths of insight and experience their music holds.

Lest we think the problem is limited to the Euro-American Protestant tradition, Taiwanese theologian and musician I-to Loh observes that "the wholesale importation of Western praise choruses and pop style hymns is causing a host of problems [in Taiwan and Asia]. The people's musical ability has declined. . . . Native traditions and newly composed songs in ethnic styles have little chance of survival."[15]

I know that keeping traditional sacred music, whatever its roots, alive and well in our churches is not easy. I also acknowledge that contemporary praise music is far more popular, as witnessed by the explosion of megachurch music.

However, I think it's important to ask if we would give up other parts of our ministry and tradition because they're not popular. Would we forego our advocacy for human rights or our freedom of thought and belief? Our passion for the oppressed or our commitment to social justice issues?

None of those things make us popular nor guarantee our churches will grow. Yet we are committed to those expressions of our faith. Why then would we let the music of our tradition be swallowed up in the tidal wave of music that is as homogeneous as the culture from which it derives?

The music of our worship should remind us both of the God of the ages and also of the people in every age who have given voice to their faith in song. So, why not "jazz, rock, *and* J. S. Bach"?

Sacred Music Reminds Us That God Is Still Speaking—and Singing

Pastor John Robinson told the Pilgrims as they headed to what was for them a new world, "God hath yet more light and truth to break forth from (the) Holy Word."[16] More often than not, that light and truth break forth in song.

Having just argued the case for the church's heritage of classical and traditional music, I also would advocate being open to "singing a new song—or several—to the Lord" in worship. We believe in a God of continuing revelation, and that needs to be reflected in our music as well. Just as we need to know the songs that have given people hope throughout the ages, we also need to know what contemporary music gives that hope now.

I once asked a young woman who performed nightly at a local cabaret to sing for Palm Sunday and left the choice of music up to her. She chose "What I Did for Love" from *A Chorus Line*. You won't find it in *The New Century Hymnal*. But for her, along with others in the congregation, that Broadway ballad expressed what Jesus did in Holy Week as much as "O Sacred Head Now Wounded" did for others.

So listen to the music of the world around you and your congregation, and be open to new expressions of sacred music, from both inside and outside the church. All "traditional" or classical music was new at one time, and composers as famous as Mozart and Handel got themselves in trouble for introducing new sounds in sacred places.

As a pastor for a relatively new UCC congregation, I know that for decades church growth experts have often advocated a homogeneous approach to music in worship. This "birds of a feather sing together" approach encourages congregations to develop separate "contemporary" and perhaps "traditional" services. In recent years, however, leaders like Tom Long and others advocate blending the two styles, into what Long describes as "eclectic excellence."[17]

As you can tell from this chapter, I come down on the side of eclectic excellence. I certainly want our churches to grow, but homogeneity in music isn't a faithful way to insure that. God is far more imaginative, and the people of God far more diverse, than can be expressed or experienced in any one style, generation, culture, or era of music.

When it comes to sacred music, I'm a firm believer in the Julia Child school of thought. "Go hog wild when you cook," proclaimed the famous chef. "Use all the pots and pans."[18] I encourage you to do the same.

And if—or when—disagreements arise, just remember that the great cloud of witnesses surrounding us didn't always see eye to eye, or hear ear to ear either!

Whatever music you do in worship, enjoy it. Let it take you to the heights and depths of the human experience and of your relationship with God. Let music heal you, comfort you, challenge you, and strengthen you. Let it continually reveal something of God's mystery and power to you.

In other words, whatever your congregation's musical voice, sing "Alleluia" and keep on walking.

Nine

Friends and Neighbors: Being the Worshipping Community

We are in search of each other as well as of Thee in this act of worship. . . . May Thy Presence invade our being until at last there begins to stir within us that which breaks the circle, spilling over into the lives of each other and we are no longer alone.

—Howard Thurman[1]

You really can't run the river solo. Well, you can, but it's not advised. Besides it would be pretty lonely. All that beauty and no one to say "wow" with? No one to bear witness with you?

You really can't worship solo either. Well, you can, but after a while there's that loneliness factor. Apart from our human need for community, there's good biblical basis for worship being communal. The one and only prayer Jesus taught his disciples doesn't have an "I" in it. "Give *us* this day *our* daily bread."

On some level most of us get it. Ask people why they go to church, and community tops the list. Of course, knowing we *like* community is different than actually *being* community. A worshipping community isn't just a concept; it's a living, breathing reality that has to be re-created every Sunday morning. And that can be a challenge.

Just getting people to show up can be daunting—as any pastor, youth leader, choir director, or greeter coordinator can verify. For one, our Sabbathless 24/7 world often leaves Sunday morning as the only time to be with family or do laundry before it all starts over again. Two, in the lingo of cultural anthropologists, church has become a "third place"—a community, behind family and work, where, in the song of the old TV series *Cheers*, "everybody knows your name and they're always glad you came." But there's a lot of competition for "third place," from Sunday hockey leagues to hiking clubs to brunch at Applebees. More often than not, worship comes in last place. Three, our culture encourages the belief that spirituality is a private affair and organized religion an object of mistrust.

I wish I had a magic wand to change these realities. It is discouraging to have the life-giving gift of Christian worship become a take-it-or-leave-it commodity in our culture. And there is little that makes me think more un-Christian thoughts than to have someone tell me they don't need church to "be spiritual."

I don't have that wand, but here are some suggestions as to "gather the people." Reuben Sheares offered a unique way when he was the pastor for Park Manor Congregational Church on the southside of Chicago. One December, he told me he was baptizing his first grandchild the Sunday after Christmas. I was surprised the baptism was on such a "low Sunday." Reuben replied that was precisely why they were doing it. "In the African American church," he said, "you better believe people show up if the preacher's grandbaby is being baptized." He was right. Park Manor had more people the Sunday after Christmas that year than on Christmas Eve.

In case you don't have children or the ones you do have aren't producing grandchildren on schedule yet, you may want to explore some other possibilities:

Get the Word Out

Regular, consistent, and interesting publicity in a variety of settings is vital. Local congregations need to take seriously our culture's stereotypes, generally negative, about church and Christianity. We may see our worship services as progressive, fun, welcoming, and liberating, but thanks to the media, most people won't share that perception unless we also use the media to paint a different picture.

In some communities, getting that publicity is fairly easy. In Santa Fe, the local paper devotes two pages weekly to faith community news, from

Orthodox Christian to Calvary Chapel to Wiccan. We make sure we're on the page, too.

However, in many communities, newspapers and other media offer little access to local churches. Moreover, fewer people read traditional newspapers and surf the web instead. Developing and maintaining an informative, engaging *website* is crucial if a congregation wants people beyond its walls to know about it. Yes, it costs money. But a website with lots of pictures can capture the spirit of a worshipping congregation far better than any newspaper ad or article.

Website or advertising may get the church "well-branded" with more people "checking us out." But unless the church behind the publicity has something to offer—namely, a vibrant soul-filled and soul-feeding worshipping community—people may come once or twice, but won't stick around to become part of the community.

Creating a catchy ad campaign or jazzy website is one thing. Creating a sense of commitment in the people who come is totally another.

Get People Engaged

Once people show up, get them thinking about worship the other six days of the week. That may seem obvious, but it has to be intentional. Here are some ways I've found that work:

Sermon series with particular themes to build interest from one Sunday to the next. Sometimes those themes come from the text themselves, like a series on "Law and Grace" when the lectionary was Romans or "Who Is This Jesus?" derived from the Lenten Gospel texts. Other times, current events can provide a theme, such as a series on "Building Hope in a Fearful Time."

Our music director and pianist offers a similar "serial" approach with the service music. For the 250th anniversary of Mozart's birth, the month's preludes and postludes were his compositions. The month of July is often a time of American music, starting on Independence Day.

Whether for sermons or music, series make people feel they are going to miss out on something important if they miss worship.

Get the word out between Sundays. In your newsletter and/or web page, include a worship page with the theme for the season and each Sunday's sermon title and weekly texts, along with a brief description of how you're going to engage the text or the questions it raises. Each week, I also send an e-mail to the congregation with that Sunday's information, including a slightly longer introduction to the text and/or theme. It can plant seeds of thought and curiosity about worship before people ever come through the doors.

I include what the children are doing in children's church and the music—hymns, songs, and anthems as well as prelude and postlude. Adults often come because of what's offered for children and what music they'll hear.

Bible study for sermon preparation. It helps to have some other minds, hearts, and souls engage the Scripture texts for the sermon. Sometimes that takes the form of an ongoing study group with whomever is interested from the congregation. Other times, I've specifically asked certain groups to study with me for a period of time, like a four-week study with lawyers on the Letter to the Romans or a gathering of doctors and nurses to explore the healing miracles. Another way is to e-mail the congregation on Monday with the text and ask people to write back what questions or insights they have about the Scripture.

People have a stake in the service if they've helped the preacher prepare. They'll come to find out what *you* did with their ideas.

Be intentional about being inclusive. People will show up to be the worshipping community if we ask them to show up for leadership. One of our goals is to have a number of voices—men and women, girls and boys, youth, older persons—be heard in worship. That diversity isn't reflected in every service, but over the course of a season or a year, we try to include many people in many leadership roles.

Even if a person never wants to be "up front" in worship, seeing and hearing a variety of people share leadership lets them see there is a place in the community for everyone, including them.

Help People "Learn the Ropes"

Go back to the river trip with me for just a moment. As I wrote earlier, I had wanted to take a trip like that all my life. But by the fourth day, if I could have hiked out, I probably would have. Why? Because it felt like everyone else knew what they were doing and I didn't have a clue. In the most awesome place in the world, I was focused on reorganizing my dry bag, figuring out how to get my teeth brushed, and castigating myself for bringing too many books. Before I could enter into the experience, I had to deal with my disorientation and sense of being the outsider.

Thanks to lots of encouragement from the group leader and others, I began to catch on. When I did, a new world began to open up. The language, the rhythms, and even rituals of the river began to make sense.

The people who come through our doors for worship may well need that same kind of shepherding. They can have the same questions and doubts I faced on the river: "Am I going to fit in? Will I know what to do? How come everyone else seems so comfortable here?" Whether people are coming from UCC backgrounds, other traditions, or no church experience, we need to help them "learn the ropes" of worship in our particular congregations.

Try to make worship "user-friendly." By that I don't meaning dumbing down to the lowest common denominator. Nor do I mean rejecting symbols that may make people uncomfortable but that are deeply rooted in the Christian tradition, like the cross, or liturgy, like the morning offering.

What I do mean is reframing such symbols or practices in ways that are life-giving. For example, I often preface the call to confession with Frederick Buechner's understanding of the word (either printed in bulletin and/or spoken before the prayer): "To confess our sins is not to tell God something God doesn't already know. But until we confess them, they are the abyss between God and us. When we confess them, they become the bridge."[2]

"Unpack" the music of a service, too. When people come to a church, they enter a musical world quite different from their radio or their iPod. Sometimes we include in the bulletin or sermon the background of a particular hymn or anthem, to set it in context or help explain it, just as we do with Scripture in the sermon.

Rest assured, worship at United is not one continual explanation of what we're doing and why. Rather these suggestions are used intermittently to create an overall environment in worship that affirms our desire to include both new people and ongoing members in the community.

Provide opportunities outside the worship services, such as Sunday forums or retreats, to help the congregation understand *why* you do what you do in worship, *how* you do it, and *why* it matters. Our responsibility as worship leaders is to create a worshipping community that meets people where they are, helps them know what they need to know, and challenges them to enter a new world.

Remember What—and Who—Calls You Together

When it comes to community, there was one crucial difference between the river trip and Sunday worship. Once we put in at Lee's Ferry, we were pretty much stuck with each other for the rest of the trip. In the church, it's a lot easier to bail.

The music that makes my heart sing doesn't do a thing for you. You believe that the preacher needs to be a prophet and take a political stand. I think we need to keep politics and religion separate. I like to pray out loud during intercessory prayer. You think people should keep their troubles and their prayers to themselves. You say trespasses. I say debts. Tomato, tomahto, potato, potahto. Let's call the whole thing off.

The reason we don't is because of other things we also do together in worship. We share a meal and a story about twelve very different people, all very scared, with very different ideas about the person who led the meal, all very welcomed to the table by that same person. If Jesus could not only put up with those twelve disciples, but love them to the very end, then maybe we can continue to try to do so with one another (even if your taste in music could use some work).

By no means do I minimize the very real conflicts over music, liturgy, and just about everything else that afflict many of our congregations these days. But even as we acknowledge what pulls us apart in the Christian church, it's important to remember what draws us together—like the bread, the cup, and the One who calls us into worship to share that feast.

As stated in the chapter on the elements of worship, at United, we also do something else together in worship. Even those Sundays when we don't eat together, we breathe together. What started as a purely practical way to get people centered for worship now reminds us that that we all depend on one God. Despite our differences of opinion, musical taste, or even belief, we consciously draw upon the same breath from the same God—the God who loves you, me, and everyone else who showed up that morning.

Finally, we also try to listen together. To listen to God in the same silence and speaking through the same Scripture. To listen to God in the music, even if it's not our style. To listen to God in prayer.

Like the bread, the cup, and breath itself, prayer in worship can remind us, often through the "sighs too deep for words," of our common need for God. If someone asks us to pray for a dying loved one or a wayward child, we don't question if they are a "seeker" or "believer" or who they voted for in the last election before we respond, "Lord, hear our prayer." In prayer, we remember there is no such thing as "traditional grief" and "contemporary grief," Republican grief or Democratic grief.

As a community of faith, despite our differences—or more accurately, *because* of them—we don't just talk to one another. We intentionally listen to one another to know better what holds meaning for them, to hear what's on their heart.

We also ask that they listen to us. We take the risk of talking to God with the congregation overhearing, telling both God and our neighbors what's important to us, what's on our hearts and minds, too.

Such deep listening is a radical thing to do in our world of sound bites, text messaging, and polarization of issues. But when we make the commitment to be a worshipping community, there's no telling what God might reveal to us. Bill was a homeless man who lived in the arroyo near United and who started coming to church one fall. Bill always wore earphones, so I never knew if he actually heard anything other than his radio. It was hard to tell if he was simply very shy or had a mental illness that kept him from being able to relate with other people. Over time, he began to come early to help set up tables for the summer breakfasts or sweep the front sidewalk.

He came to worship, but seemed uncomfortable and always sat in the back, never coming forward for Communion and leaving before the final hymn. To be honest, I wondered if joining in worship was simply a way to get out of the cold.

Then came the Sunday after Christmas 2004. I had just offered the pastoral prayer and we were in the time of intercessory prayer. My eyes closed and my head bowed, I was about to start the Lord's Prayer, when I heard Bill's voice from the back of the sanctuary. "For the hundred or more people," he prayed aloud, "who have lost their lives in the tidal wave. Lord, in your mercy." As the congregation responded, "Hear our prayer," I wondered what he was referring to. In the coffee hour, Bill told me that during the sermon he had heard on his radio about a huge wave that had hit Indonesia. It was the first we learned of the devastating tsunami that took hundreds of thousands of lives in South Asia. Thanks to Bill's prayer, we held them in prayer even before we knew what had happened.

Being the worshipping community is often a challenge. It's also far more than just a "third place" to hang out. God always seems to have a way of speaking to us through the friends, neighbors, strangers, and all the others who've come to worship, just like us.

Ten

Hope Is a Muscle:
Keeping Worship Vital

Lord, you bless the words assuring,
"I am with you to the end."
Faith and hope and love restoring,
May we serve you as you intend.
And, amid the cares that claim us,
Hold in mind eternity;
With the Spirit's gifts empow'r us
For the work of ministry.

—Jeffery Rowthorn[1]

f I had one regret about the river trip, it was that I had not prepared physically. Generally, I'm a pretty strong hiker and feel at home in the outdoors. But too many night meetings, staff changes, deaths, and funerals meant too few hikes or trips to the gym. On the trip, my innate stubbornness got me farther than I thought I could go, but there were things I simply couldn't do—a rock wall I couldn't scale, a hike to a waterfall I had to forego.

Everything I had done in the months prior to the trip was important ministry. But I hadn't made preparation an ongoing priority. I paid for it in sore muscles and not having the strength to do what I wanted to do. How can you *not* hike to a waterfall?

In the United Church of Christ, we want to do a lot of things—from feeding the hungry to advocating for economic justice. Our congregations build Habitat houses and tutor low-income school children. When there is a tsunami in South Asia or starvation in Darfur, we work to raise money for the victims and raise consciousness about the underlying causes of the tragedy. In our daily lives of work and raising children, we believe our faith challenges to make ethical decisions and care about justice.

We do all this because we believe in our bones that being a Christian means following in the way of the One who gave his life for others. We believe the prophet Micah had it right when he said, "What does the Lord require of you but to do justice, and to love kindness and to walk humbly with your God?" (Micah 6:8).

That justice ministry can be as arduous as hiking any canyon and as scary as running any rapid. Sometimes it's plain hard work, hard on the heart and hard on the soul.

"Hope is a muscle," affirms the title of a book about a girls' basketball team.[2] It has to be exercised, renewed, and restored. So do our other muscles of faith and love. In the Christian church, the primary place we do that is in worship—regular, enlivening, energizing, vital worship.

Not getting in shape for the river trip sometimes left me exhausted, fearful I couldn't keep up, and unable to do things I wanted to do. Not keeping worship a fundamental priority in our churches, locally and nationally, will leave us with diminishing membership, energy, and resources. No matter how much I wanted to hike to Seven Springs, I didn't have the physical stamina to do it. No matter how much we care about justice and outreach, or how right we believe our cause to be, if we haven't gathered our congregations in a strong, ongoing worship life, we will not have the inner resources to do what we believe God is calling us to do.

As Jeffery Rowthorn states, "The world needs us to be strong in the faith. Vital worship is needed to build vital, sturdy Christians, especially if you are to live into the social justice ministries of your tradition in the United Church of Christ."[3] Rowthorn knows of what he speaks. A former Anglican/Episcopal bishop of Europe and professor of worship, he taught and worked with UCC and other Reformed Protestants students at Union Theological School and then Yale Divinity School for almost twenty years. He has the utmost respect for our traditions, especially for the UCC's commitment to social justice and peace. He tells the story of celebrating the Eucharist at Union in the late 1960s, and afterward seeing some of the seminarians leave to go turn in their drafts cards. "There was an immediate connection," he says, "between the story and ritual of God's sacrifice for us and a response of sacrifice and discipleship."

"If we are to engage the powers and principalities of our world with vitality and strength," Rowthorn affirms, "we need worship with vitality and strength."[4]

I hope throughout this book you have found ways to develop and maintain the vitality and strength of worship in your congregation through the particular elements of music, the sacraments, structure, and preaching.

Of course, the primary way is to do what I didn't do for the river trip: *Keep worship a priority.*

As Reuben Sheares reminded me as a young minister, "That one hour of worship will shape their lives, their faith, and their life together more than anything else you do. Keep it central. Don't take it for granted. Give it your absolute best."[5]

That one hour a week of worship demands hours of preparation: practice time for musicians, sermon writing time for preachers, set-up time for liturgical arts. But we also need time to step back from the everyday demands to explore the larger picture of worship, engage people in conversation, and experience new music or other worship forms.

If you're a lay leader, see your role beyond that of ordering the palms for Holy Week or arranging the liturgist schedule. Keep learning as much as you can about worship. Assist your pastor in organizing forums or retreats on worship. Help create an environment in your church that values worship, explores tradition, and is open to new possibilities.

As importantly, advocate for the staff, both paid and volunteer, your church needs to insure vital worship. That means not only pastoral or music staff, but also sufficient administrative and custodial support. Your pastor can't be the worship leader you've called him or her to be if they are spending time typing the bulletin, recruiting ushers, or being the building manager. If your pastor is to develop and lead vital worship, she or he needs time to think, read, explore, and plan. Be an advocate for that kind of time and for the staffing and other resources it requires.

If you are a pastor, set the example and keep worship as the center of your ministry, from which everything else flows. That one hour a week is the most important hour of your ministry. I know how overwhelming the other parts of our work can be, from pastoral care to outreach work to fundraising. I also know how our worship life strengthens those ministries. If people experience God's abundant presence in worship, they are more likely to act with abundant faith and hope in the ministries to which we challenge them, whether it's working for justice and peace or faithfully and generously supporting the stewardship campaign.

Time and again, I've seen the "fruits of our worship" in the daily ministries of the congregation. The public school teacher who keeps a copy of our benediction on her refrigerator door as a reminder of her "marching orders" before she faces 180 eighth graders every day. The young woman who, when her father was in a coma and her fears blocked her prayers, remembered how in worship we breathe in God's gifts and so used that to keep the demons at bay as she kept vigil at the hospital. The young man who drives forty miles to church every week and sits in the sanctuary before services listening to the choir. "It doesn't just get me through the week," he says. "It helps me be the person I want to be, especially when I'm facing ethical dilemmas at work or trying to keep the peace among the people I supervise."[6]

So as a pastor, take your leadership of worship seriously, but not so seriously that worship isn't lively or engaging, for you as well as for the congregation. Do a periodic "joy check." If worship is leaving you cold, it may be time to get out of Dodge for a while. If after a break, you still dread Sunday mornings, then you might want to have a good talk with God—or a trusted colleague. God may well be calling you to a different form of ministry.

Two final lessons from the river. One, eighteen days after we put our rafts in at Lee's Ferry, we took them out for the last time at Diamond Creek. The rest of the group went back to Santa Fe, but I drove up to the South Rim for a couple days. I wasn't ready to leave the canyon yet.

I checked out every lookout point to get a glimpse of the river I'd just left. I couldn't resist telling other tourists, "I've just come from there. I've been in those rapids, camped on that delta."

Vital worship can create that same kind of longing to stay connected and the hunger to share the experience. Like the river trip, each service ends and we return to the world. But as the river trip reminded me, we can carry the experience of worship into the other six days of the week, even into the rest of our lives.

A second lesson from the river. As soon as I got back to Santa Fe, I took my film to be developed. I'd shot twenty rolls on the trip, and even borrowed a wide-angle lens to make sure I could capture the canyon's vast beauty. I couldn't wait to get the pictures back.

But when I picked them up, I realized what every photographer learns sooner or later about the Grand Canyon. No matter how wide your lens or how many pictures you take, you simply can't capture it. Too many layers and vistas, too much depth, too many changes of light, shadow, and color. The photos offered memories, to be sure, but no one picture nor even a series of pictures could embody a fraction of the experience.

I think we can experience the same frustration as leaders of worship. We try our hardest, plan, pray, hope, explore, and still can't connect to the eternal mystery and power we know exists. It's too vast, too deep, too eternal. Sometimes we don't even come close.

But we keep trying, because there are times it does happen. When worship does come together, and you and your congregation together touch the promised "wonder, love, and praise." Trust those times, because that's what you've been called to.

That's the goal, our job as preachers, pastors, and leaders of local churches.

So when the ushers don't show up, the candles don't get lit, there's a crying baby in the midst of the sermon, and afterward someone in line tells you, "It just didn't work for me today," hold fast to your call. As Jeffery Rowthorn writes, "Hold in mind eternity." [7]

And in those other times? When what happens in worship seems light years from what you know *could* happen? Just remember—the Grand Canyon wasn't formed in a day or even a lifetime. Neither was the worship of the Christian church nor our part of it. The river took eons of time to carve the beauty of the canyon. It's still doing its work.

Similarly it has taken millennia for God's powerful, flowing Spirit to shape the life and worship of the Christian church. That Spirit still shapes us, if we trust it.

Let your commitment to vital worship be as consistent as that river. Who knows what ministries will be shaped, what sublime mysteries and deep hopes will be carved in the life of your congregation—and in your life—by the vital river of life we call worship.

"A river touches places of which its source knows nothing."

—Oswald Chambers[8]

Notes

Introduction

1. Jeffery Rowthorn, "Lord, You Give the Great Commission." *The Hymnal 1982* (New York: Church Publishing, 1985), #528. © 1978 Hope Publishing Company, Carol Stream, IL 60188. All rights reserved. Used by permission.

2. Frederick Buechner, *Wishful Thinking: A Theological ABC* (New York: HarperCollins, 1973), 98.

3. Luke Calhoun, Personal e-mail correspondence, August 27, 2006. Used by permission.

Chapter One

1. Abraham Heschel, *I Asked for Wonder* (New York: Crossroad Publishing Company, 1988), 2.

2. Evelyn Underhill, *Worship* (New York: Harper and Brothers, 1937), 3.

3. Heschel, *I Asked for Wonder*, 2.

Chapter Two

1. Underhill, *Worship*, 81.

2. "De Colores (Sing of Colors)," *The New Century Hymnal* (Cleveland: Pilgrim Press, 1995), #402. English translation ©1995 by The Pilgrim Press. Used by permission. All rights reserved.

3. The four categories outlined in pp. 27–28 were defined by the Nairobi Statement on Worship, developed by the World Council of Churches in 1996. They are delineated by C. Michael Hawn in "Singing with the

Faithful in Every Time and Place: Thoughts on Liturgical Inculturation and Cross-Cultural Liturgy," *Colloquium: Music, Worship, Arts,* (Yale Institute of Sacred Music) Vol. 2 (Autumn 2005): 109–10.

4. Elliot Forbes, "Randall Thompson," *Harvard Magazine* 103, no. 6 (July–August 2001), http://www.harvardmagazine.com/on-line/070181.html.

Chapter Three

1. Kenneth Grahame, *The Wind in the Willows* (New York: HarperCollins Publishers, 2003), 7–8.

2. Richard R. Hammar, *Church and Clergy Tax Guide, 2007 edition* (Carol Spring, IL: Christianity Today, 2006), 413.

3. Marva Dawn, *A Royal Waste of Time: The Splendor of Worshipping God and Being Church for the World* (Grand Rapids: Eerdmans, 2000).

4. Reuben A. Sheares, III, Personal conversation, January 31, 1989.

5. Anne Morrow Lindbergh, *Gift from the Sea* (New York: Pantheon Books, 1997), 29.

6. Ibid., 23.

7. e. e. cummings, "i thank You God for most this amazing," in *Complete Poems: 1904–1962,* edited by George J. Firmage (New York: Liveright Publishing Corporation, 1979), 65.

8. Toni Morrison, *Beloved* (New York: Alfred A. Knopf, 1987), 87–89.

9. Ibid.

10. Underhill, *Worship,* 5.

11. Peggy V. Beck, and Anna Lee Walters, *The Sacred: Ways of Knowledge, Sources of Life* (Tsaile, AZ: Navajo Community College Press, 1977), 13.

12. Maria Hamilton, Confirmation paper for the United Church of Santa Fe, Feb., 2000, p. 2. Used by permission.

13. Lindbergh, *Gift from the Sea,* 114–15.

14. Beck and Walters, *The Sacred,* 30.

15. Buechner, *Wishful Thinking,* 18.

16. Morrison, *Beloved,* 273.

Chapter Four

1. Mato-Kuwapi, quoted in *Touch the Earth.* edited by T. C. McLuhan (New York: Promotory Press, 1971), 35.

2. Ella Natonabah Jones, Personal conversation, February 1997. Used by permission.

3. Yvonne Delk, "The World as God Intends," *Sojourners,* no. 3 (May–

June 1999): 18–23.

4. Fred Craddock, The Earl Lectures (Berkeley, CA: Pacific School of Religion, January 1990). Used by permission.

5. Beck and Walters, *The Sacred*, 23.

6. Harry E. Fosdick, "God of Grace and God of Glory," *The New Century Hymnal* (Cleveland: Pilgrim Press, 1995), #436.

7. Steven Smith, Personal interview with author. April 2006. Used by permission.

8. Beck and Walters, *The Sacred*, 23.

9. Willimon, *Worship as Pastoral Care* (Nashville: Abingdon, 1979), 216.

10. Ibid., 217.

11. Jeffery Rowthorn, Personal interview, August 17, 2006. Used by permission.

Chapter Five

1. May Sarton, "Santos: New Mexico," in *Collected Poems (1930–1973)* (New York: Norton, 1974), 60. Reprinted by the permission of Russell and Volkening as agents for the author. Copyright © 1938 by May Sarton. Copyright renewed 1966 by May Sarton.

2. Ibid., 60.

3. "Come, O Come Emmanuel," *The New Century Hymnal* (Cleveland: Pilgrim Press, 1995), #116.

4. Sarton, "Santos: New Mexico," 60.

5. John Bowring, "Watcher, Tell Us of the Night," *The New Century Hymnal* (Cleveland: Pilgrim Press, 1995), #103.

6. "Prayer for the First Sunday in Advent," *Lutheran Book of Worship* (Minneapolis: Augsburg Publishing House, 1978), 13.

7. Madeleine L'Engle, *The Irrational Season* (New York: Seabury Press, 1976), 27.

8. A paraphrase of Ina Hughes's "A Prayer for Children," in *Guide My Feet*, ed. Marion Wright Edelman (Boston: Beacon Press, 1995), 106–8. Used by permission.

9. Tony Robinson, Personal e-mail, April 12, 2007. Used by permission.

10. Christian History Institute, "Glimpses #147: Messiah and Georg Frederic Handel," 2007, http://chi.gospelcom.net.

11. Barbara Kingsolver, *High Tide in Tucson* (New York: HarperPerennial, 1996), 15.

12. Wendell Berry, "So, Friends, Every Day Do Something," in *Earth*

Prayers, ed. Elizabeth Roberts and Elias Amidon, 123 (San Francisco: HarperSanFrancisco, 1991).

13. John Wesley Powell, "The Exploration of the Colorado River and its Canyons: 1895," in *Down the Great Unknown: John Wesley Powell's "1869 Journey of Discovery and Tragedy through the Grand Canyon,"* edited by Edwin Dolnick, 262–63 (London: Harper Collins, 2001).

14. Sarton, "Santos: New Mexico," 60.

Chapter Six

1. Morrison, *Beloved,* 272–73.

2. Paul Tillich, *The New Being* (New York: Charles Scribner's Sons, 1955), 18.

3. John Robinson, 1620 sermon to Pilgrims as they left Europe for New England, http://www.ucc.org/about-us/firsts.html.

4. Frederick Buechner, *Telling the Truth: The Gospel as Tragedy, Comedy, and Fairy Tale* (San Francisco: Harper and Row, 1977), 8–14, 50–53.

5. Tony Robinson, "The Courage to Preach," in *The Source: Newsletter of the Church Council of Greater Seattle* (October 2006): 1. Used by permission of the author.

6. Marilynn Robinson, *Gilead* (New York: Farrar, Straus, Giroux, 2004), 45.

7. Francis of Assisi, quoted in St. Antony of Padua: A Biographical and Critical Study, Chapter 4: "Reading Theology to the Brothers", http://paulspilsbury.users.btopenworld.com/LIFE4.htm

8. Roger Repohl, quoted by Martin Marty, "Be Still," *Context* 38, no. 5 (May 2006): 1.

Chapter Seven

1. e. e. cummings, "i thank You God for most this amazing," 65. Copyright 1950, ©1978, 1991 by the Trustees for the E.E. Cummings Trust. Copyright © 1979 by George James Firmage, from *Complete Poems: 1904–1962* by E. E. Cummings, edited by George J. Firmage. Used by permission of the Liveright Publishing Corporation.

2. cummings, "i thank You God for most this amazing," 65.

3. "Sacrament," *Webster's New Collegiate Dictionary* (Springfield, IL: G. & C. Merriam, 1975).

4. cummings, "i thank You God for most this amazing," 65.

5. Ronald Cole-Turner, "Child of Blessing, Child of Promise," *The New*

Century Hymnal (Cleveland: Pilgrim Press, 1995), #325.

6. Willimon, *Worship as Pastoral Care*, 157.

7. Charles A. Tindley, "We Are Often Tossed and Driven," *The New Century Hymnal* (Cleveland: Pilgrim Press, 1995), #444.

8. This story about his father and the song "Bye and Bye" was one Reuben Sheares told often in a variety of settings in the United Church of Christ. I first heard it at a meeting of the Directorate of the Office for Church Life and Leadership in 1983.

9. "Service of Word and Sacrament I," in the *Book of Worship: United Church of Christ* (New York: United Church of Christ Office for Church Life and Leadership, 1986), 44.

Chapter Eight

1. John Wesley Powell, quoted in Susan Lamb, *Grand Canyon: The Vault of Heaven* (Grand Canyon, AZ: Grand Canyon Association, 1995), 61.

2. Joseph Gilineau, "Music and Singing in the Liturgy," in *The Study of Liturgy*, ed. Cheslyn Jones et al., 440. (New York: Oxford University Press, 1978).

3. Augustine of Hippo, quoted in "Sermon for the 6th Sunday of Easter" by James B. Lemler, May 4, 2002, http://www.day1.net

4. Carol Doran, and Thomas H. Troeger, *Trouble at the Table: Gathering the Tribes for Worship* (Nashville: Abingdon, 1992), 68–69.

5. From a movie review of "Amandla! A Revolution in Four Part Harmony," Director Lee Hirsch. Review by Jamie Russell for http://www.bbc.co.uk, November 28, 2003.

6. Interview with Lee Hirsch by David Haviland for "Songs of the Struggle" from http://www.eyeforfilm.o.uk/feature.

7. Doran and Troeger, *Trouble at the Table*, 71.

8. Underhill, *Worship*, 3.

9. Doran and Troeger, *Trouble at the Table*, 37.

10. David S. Lovejoy, *Religious Enthusiasm in the Great Awakening* (Englewood Cliffs, NJ: Prentice Hall, 1969), 5.

11. Brian Wren, "Bring Many Names," *The New Century Hymnal* (Cleveland: Pilgrim Press, 1995), #11. © 1989 Hope Publishing Company, Carol Stream, IL 60188. All rights reserved. Used by permission.

12. John Bell, "Sing a New Song," *The Christian Century* 123, no. 15 (July 25, 2006): 21.

13. Ibid.

14. Gustavo Guiterriez, "Conversion to the Neighbor," in *A Theology of Liberation*, 194–203 (Maryknoll, NY: Orbis Books, 1973).

15. I-to Loh, "Contextualization vs. Globalization: A Glimpse of Sounds and Symbols in Asian Worship," in *Colloquium: Music, Worship, Arts* (Yale Institute of Sacred Music) 2 (Autumn 2005): 125.

16. Robinson, 1620 sermon to Pilgrims, http://www.ucc.org/about-us/firsts.html.

17. Thomas Long expands on this idea in his *Beyond the Worship Wars: Building Vital and Faithful Worship* (Herndon, VA: Alban Institute, 2001).

18. Julia Child, quoted in segment 4, http://prairiehome.publicradio.org/programs/2004/09/04

Chapter Nine

1. Howard Thurman, *The Centering Moment* (New York: Harper and Row, 1969), 65.

2. Buechner, *Telling the Truth*, 15.

Chapter Ten

1. Jeffery Rowthorn, "Lord, You Give the Great Commission," *The Hymnal 1982* (New York: Church Publishing, 1985), #528. © 1978 Hope Publishing Company, Carol Stream, IL 60188. All rights reserved. Used by permission.

2. Madeleine Blaise, *In These Girls, Hope Is a Muscle* (New York: Grand Central Publishing, 1996).

3. Jeffery Rowthorn, Personal interview, August 17, 2006. Used by permission.

4. Ibid.

5. Reuben Sheares, Personal conversation, January 31, 1987.

6. Personal conversation, July 25, 2007.

7. Rowthorn, 528.

8. Oswald Chambers, *My Utmost for His Highest* (Uhrichsville, OH: Barbour Publishing, 1963), September 6.